THE
LORNA DOONE TRAIL

THE
LORNA DOONE TRAIL

Text by R.D. Blackmore
Selection and Commentary by S.H. Burton,
Revised and expanded by
John Burgess and Caroline Tonson-Rye

First printed in 2018

This selection from Lorna Doone, Introduction and Commentary
© S.H. Burton 1975, John Burgess, Carline Tonson-Rye 2018

British Library Cataloguing-in-Publication Data
A CIP record for this title is available from the
British Library

ISBN 978 0 85710 121 1
PiXZ Books
Halsgrove House, Ryelands Business Park,
Bagley Road, Wellington, Somerset TA21 9PZ
Tel: 01823 653777
Fax: 01823 216796
email: sales@halsgrove.com

An imprint of Halstar Ltd, part of the
Halsgrove group of companies
Information on all Halsgrove titles is
available at: www.halsgrove.com

Printed and bound by Parksons Graphics, India

Contents

Acknowledgements

Our thanks go to the following for advice and help: Dr Sue Baker, the Exmoor Society, Molly Groves, the staff at Tiverton Museum, and Mike Sampson.

Many of the photographs were taken by John Burgess. We are grateful to David Austen for permission to photograph the Old Forge, Brendon; the staff at Barnstaple Museum for permission to photograph Tom Faggus's gun; the Rev. Colin Burke for permission to reproduce the photographs of Oare Church; Nigel and Hazel Binding, Yenworthy Farm, for permission to photograph the farmhouse and the long gun and, together with Richard and Christine Binding, for posing for the cover photograph; Robert and Sue Pile, Coombe Farm, for allowing us to photograph their farmyard; and the Woollacott family for permission to photograph Oareford Farm. We also thank Elizabeth Robinson for permission to print her drawing of packhorses; and the Exmoor National Park Authority and Paul Savage for permission to reproduce their photographs.

Lynmouth

Valley of
Rocks

Malmsmead

Brendon   Oare

A39

Porlock

Minehead

DOONE
COUNTRY

EXMOOR
NATIONAL PARK

Dunster

Exford

Wheddon
Cross

Simonsbath

R. Exe

Withypool

R. Barle

Tarr Steps

North Molton

Dulverton

Exebridge

A361

Bampton

South Molton

A396

Tiverton

R. Exe

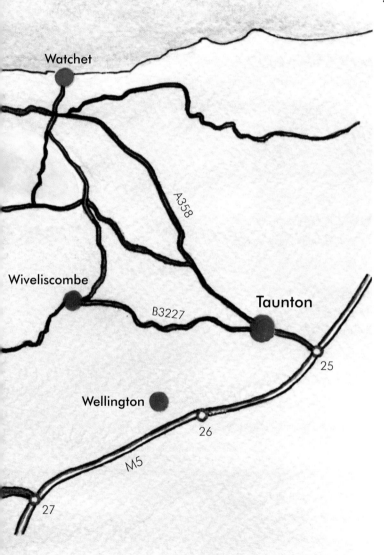

Exmoor National Park and surrounding area.

Watchet

A358

Wiveliscombe

B3227

Taunton

25

Wellington

26

M5

27

Introduction

R. D. Blackmore

'The last Victorian' – so one of his biographers (Kenneth Budd) called him. Another (W.H. Dunn) characterised him as: 'the very incarnation of England ... John Bull, with all John's virtues, idiosyncrasies, stubbornness, kindliness, touchiness, aloofness, provincialism, patriotism'. There is truth in both descriptions, but Blackmore's own assertion is more relevant to the purposes of this book: 'In everything, except the accident of birth, I am Devonian; my ancestry were all Devonians; my sympathies and feeling are all Devonian'. The explorer of the *Lorna Doone* trail will come closest to Blackmore and to an appreciation of his best-known book by seeing him in his own beloved West Country setting.

Nor will such an explorer forget what Blackmore himself was always careful to stress: Devonian though the author felt himself to be, his hero, Jan Ridd, was a yeoman and churchwarden 'of the parish of Oare, in the County of Somerset'. Blackmore's own most formative years were spent in the company of relatives to whom West Somerset was as familiar as North Devon. The modern traveller who follows Jan's adventures must cross and re-cross the meandering county boundary. 'Lorna Doone Country' is quintessential Exmoor – part in Somerset, part in Devon; and, since all the most stirring deeds described in the book take place on the moor, Blackmore could not draw – and had no wish to draw – an artificial division between the two counties.

'The accident of birth' made Blackmore a native of Longworth in North Berkshire, where his father, the Rev. John Blackmore, was Curate-in-Charge. The accident of death, together with John Blackmore's longing to return to more congenial scenes, brought the infant boy to Culmstock in East Devon. In the autumn of 1825 just three months after Blackmore's birth, an outbreak of typhus fever ravaged Longworth. Among those who died were Blackmore's mother, her twin sister, and most of the family servants.

A year later, John Blackmore accepted a curacy at Culmstock, there marrying, in 1831, his second wife – Blackmore's loved and loving stepmother – and quitting that pretty village in 1835 for Ashford, not far from Barnstaple. (Many years later, in 1894, Culmstock became the 'Perlycross' in Blackmore's novel of that name.)

The move to Ashford was indeed a homecoming. The Blackmore family traced

R.D. Blackmore in 1893 in the garden at Gomer House, Teddington, Middlesex.

its line back to the late sixteenth century when 'Richard Blackmore and Jane his wiefe' were renting land in Parracombe. John Blackmore, the novelist's grandfather, was Rector of Combe Martin and Oare. Richard, his uncle, was Rector of Charles. The Exmoor landscape was 'plotted and pieced' with Blackmore names and associations. The power of this landscape and of the family associations over an imaginative boy's mind is revealed in Blackmore's vivid reminiscence of his childhood:

> I behold an old man, with a keen profile, under a parson's shovel hat, riding a tall chestnut horse up the western slope of Exmoor, followed by his little grandson upon a shaggy and stuggy pony.

It was a family tradition, too, that took R.D. Blackmore to the West Country's most famous school. He entered Blundell's in 1837, leaving it for Exeter College, Oxford, in 1843. Later in this book the impact of his schooldays is discussed, for Blackmore, Blundell's and *Lorna Doone* are inseparable. Here, in this very brief account of his life, we can follow the course of his happy and hard-working days at Oxford. There, he was recognised as a good classical scholar and known for his quiet ways and fierce independence of mind. A contemporary remembered him as a good angler, a skilful chess player, a keen naturalist – and a good friend.

After Oxford he turned to the law and was called to the Bar in 1855. Three years later he abandoned his legal career in consequence of the epileptic attacks that now, and for some years to come, plagued him. An outdoor life was considered essential and, after filling in some years as a schoolmaster, he bought a sixteen-acre plot of land at Teddington on which he built Gomer house. Then a village, 21 miles from the centre of London, Teddington offered Blackmore that rural environment for which he craved. As W.H. Dunn pointed out, some sentences from *Clara Vaughan* (1864) accurately describe his own tastes and needs:

> Vigorous and elastic as I am, I cannot deny that the air and weather have great dominion over me. It was always so with my dear father. Two days spent indoors, without any real exercise, would make him feel as uneasy as a plant in a cellaret ... when he had lost his fishing or shooting or bit of gardening too long, he was unlike himself ... I too am not of a sedentary nature, though upon due occasion I can sit writing or drawing for some hours together. But how fine a thing all the while to see any motion outside – a leaf that can skip, or a cloud that can run! How we envy a sparrow his little hop, even across the gutter.

Teddington's proximity to the London markets was another reason for Blackmore's choice of this as his permanent home. He specialised in vegetable and fruit growing, tackling his new work with a care for detail, a patience, a determination, and an intelligence that speedily won for him renown as a horticulturalist. Unfortunately, renown butters no parsnips and, in forty years of hard and skilful work, Blackmore 'only twice made ends meet'. He attributed his lack of financial success primarily to the competition of cheap fruit imported from California.

Earlier in life Blackmore had experimented with poetry. Now, in a long battle with adversity, he turned to novel writing as a means of supplementing his income – 'I must ply the pen to pay for the spade,' he wrote to a friend. His industry was prodigious. Between 1854 and 1897 he published fourteen novels, seven volumes of verse and one volume of short stories – all this in addition to full-time labour in his market garden. In his most prolific period he averaged one long work of fiction – none of his novels is short! – every two-and-a-half years.

Today, while everybody knows of *Lorna Doone*, his other books are forgotten. Even in his lifetime, he suffered neglect from the public while enjoying the praise of some eminent critics. The truth was that he was born too late. His novels – bulky and, despite a great narrative gift in individual scenes, slow-moving – were out of fashion. The day of the three-volume novel was done – and Blackmore knew it. 'I have finished my last novel,' he said when *Dariel* came out in 1897, 'and it is high time to stop'. He was then 72 years old, tired and ill. His wife had died in 1888 after many years of indifferent health, and Blackmore felt his childless loneliness keenly. His humour and independence sustained him to the end. Who can fail to admire and love the man who, though tormented by rheumatism, could write to a friend like this?

Sad is my fate, and sad my phiz.
I am devoured with rheumatiz;
And the more I am rubbed, the worse it is.

In similar vein, he described his doctors' attempts to alleviate his condition:

What thumping fees they charged. O laws!
For 'best advice procurable'.
But now my hopes revive, because
I am pronounced incurable.

This replica memorial plaque to R.D. Blackmore is in St Mary's church, Oare. The original is in Exeter Cathedral.

He died on 20 January 1900; four years later, a memorial window and a marble portrait were dedicated to his memory in Exeter Cathedral. Words spoken at the ceremony by another famous West Country writer, Eden Phillpotts, are the fittest of epitaphs for Richard Doddridge Blackmore:

'He indicated the virtue of courage and humility, the propriety of tolerance, the value of self-reliance, the distinction of patience ... His splendid generosity, his genius for finding out the worth in others, his charity and his humour, made Blackmore a man apart ... There was in his broad sweep, like the roll of an ocean wave, something Elizabethan ... Absolutely fearless, he answered only to his own ideals, and not the most arrogant critic of literature dared to handle his work as severely as he did himself.'

Lorna Doone

The enduring popularity of *Lorna Doone* – in films, on television and in book form – may easily blind us to the fact that it sold slowly at first. Blackmore described its delayed success in his characteristically ironical way:

... *Lorna Doone* narrowly shaved the brink of Lethe. Indeed ... of the first 500 copies, only about 300 were sold ... It is the merest fluke that *Lorna Doone* was ever heard of any more ... whether from the advent of the Marquis of Lorne, or some fashionable freak, the book began to run, when on its last legs.

'The advent of the Marquis of Lorne' was one of those strokes of luck that sometimes – all-too-rarely – bring a totally unexpected windfall to an author. In

1870 Princess Louise, daughter of Queen Victoria, was betrothed to the Marquis of Lorne. Blackmore often told how a reviewer of *Lorna Doone* quite mistakenly said that the book was written about the ancestors of the Marquis – 'and then everybody read it, out of curiosity, and exhausted nearly a score of editions'.

We know now, however, that this happy mistake was by no means the real reason for the book's success. Once attention had been directed to the novel it was found to contain the essential ingredients of a best-seller; faithful love between a high-born, beautiful girl and her heroic, single-minded lover; the triumph of youth, beauty and truth over hatred, lies, oppression and cruelty; a superb villain; a wild and brilliantly delineated background; exciting deeds; suspense; humour; a strong cast of supporting characters – *Lorna Doone* has everything.

Whether the Doones ever existed or not is a complex issue, deserving (and frequently receiving) a book to itself. Here, it is sufficient to say that Blackmore did not invent the Doone legends on which he based his book (see Reading List). From childhood he had been familiar with many moorland versions of the Doone stories; familiar, too, with the various printed references to those vicious outlaws, one source of which (Thomas Henry Cooper's *Guide to Lynton*) pre-dated *Lorna Doone* by sixteen years. His own unquestioning acceptance of the Doones gave utter conviction to his writing about them. While the book was in progress he revisited Devon and Somerset. Porlock, Charles Rectory, Oare and Withypool – a copy of a signed letter from Blackmore hangs in the bar of the Royal Oak to this very day – were among the places in which he refreshed his memory, tirelessly interviewing Exmoor folk and 'putting it all down in a notebook'.

But the vividness of the style and the exuberance of the story-telling are proof enough that *Lorna Doone* came from the heart. If ever a book welled out of the dearest of a man's affections it is this. Those Exmoor days of long ago come to life in these pages: scenes, setting and story were a labour of love. As Blackmore said some years after its publication:

Nothing has pleased me more than the great success of this simple tale. For truly it is a grand success to win the attention and kind regard, not of the general public only, but also of those who are at home with the scenery, people, life and language, wherein a native cannot always satisfy the natives.

And the general public as well as the natives have gladly continued to yield their 'attention and kind regard' to this best-loved of all romances.

The Lorna Doone Story

In his preface to the first edition (1869) Blackmore himself shrewdly indicated the sources of the book's power:

> ... any son of Exmoor, chancing on this volume, cannot fail to bring to mind the nurse-tales of his childhood – the savage deeds of the Doones ... the beauty of the hapless maid brought up in the midst of them, the plain John Ridd's Herculean power, and ... the exploits of Tom Faggus, the highwayman, were – in Exmoor lore – more than mere fictions.

Set in the reigns of Charles II and James II, the novel has as its historical background Monmouth's tragic rebellion. Judge Jeffreys' fearsome personality plays a part in the story, and both John Ridd and Tom Faggus, the highwayman, were – in Exmoor lore – more than mere fictions.

Called home from Blundell's School by the news of his father's murder at the hands of the Doones, John – or Jan – Ridd devotes himself to the welfare of his mother and his sisters at Plover's Barrows Farm. A chance meeting with Lorna when he is fourteen and has made the perilous ascent into the Doone Valley colours his mind with memories of her, and puts him in possession of the secret entrance to the outlaws' fastness. When Jan is twenty-one he enters Glen Doone again, the first of a series of stolen and dangerous meetings in which he wins Lorna's heart.

The death of Sir Ensor Doone leaves Lorna unprotected, and during a great snow Jan carries her off to Plover's Barrows to save her from a forced marriage to Carver Doone. The wiles of Counsellor Doone and the savagery of Carver threaten the happiness of Jan and Lorna, but eventually it is discovered that Lorna is a direct descendant not of Sir Ensor Doone but of Scottish ancestors named Dugal. On her mother's side, she is descended from the Lords of Lorne – themselves connected by marriage with the Doones. Now her high birth and wealth interpose a barrier between Lady Lorna Dugal and the yeoman John Ridd. However, her fidelity and Jan's great services to her kinsman and Guardian in Chancery, Earl Brandir of Lochawe, ensure for the Somerset farmer signal marks of royal favour. James II knights Jan and pardons him for his innocent involvement in the Monmouth Rebellion. At Judge Jeffreys' instigation – and greatly to his profit – the rich heiress is freed from her Chancery wardship and receives royal approval for her marriage to Sir John Ridd.

Infuriated by another Doone outrage, the Exmoor people, led by Jan, finally storm the Doone Valley, only Carver escaping their just vengeance. Shortly afterwards, Jan and Lorna are married in Oare church, but Carver shoots Lorna at the altar. Believing her dead, Jan rides after the villain and brings him to bay at the Wizard's Slough. After a mighty struggle, Jan triumphs and the defeated and maddened Carver is engulfed by the fearful bog. Both Jan and Lorna recover from their wounds and live happily ever after.

The Monmouth Rebellion

Short though the Monmouth Rebellion was, it left its mark on the West Country. The following is a very brief summary of its causes and outcome.

Many of Charles II's subjects resented his rejection of parliamentary government, his acceptance of a pension from the French king, and his leaning towards the Catholic faith. As Charles had no legitimate children with his Catholic wife Catherine of Braganza (whom he married in 1662), on his death in February 1685 his Catholic brother James became king. Soon afterwards, the Duke of Monmouth (born 1649), who was the illegitimate son of Charles and Lucy Walter, decided to make a bid for the throne from his exile in Holland.

There were rumours that Charles and Lucy had married before he came to the throne in 1660 and that therefore Monmouth was legitimate. The marriage certificate was allegedly held in a 'black box', mentioned in the novel. Handsome, charming and a Protestant, the Duke had a following. But his rebellion was ill-prepared and unlucky. In less than a month of his landing at Lyme Regis in June 1685 and being proclaimed king at Taunton, he was defeated at Sedgemoor. Captured on 8 July, Monmouth was taken to London and executed on 15 July. Ironically, James II was deposed three years later and his Protestant daughter Mary and her husband William of Orange accepted the crown.

Several Assize courts tried the captured rebels. In Taunton, Judge Jeffreys passed judgement in the great hall of the Castle. Those sentenced to death were publicly hanged in towns and villages around the region to instil fear and submission. In Dunster, Dulverton and Porlock two men were hanged in each place, and in Minehead three. Other rebels were sentenced to transportation for ten years and were sold for between £10 and £15 to landowners in the West Indies. Many never returned. In the novel, this is not dwelt on, although mention is made of soldiers 'harassing the country, and hanging the people, where the rebellion had thriven' (Chapter LXVIII).

Films and TV Series

Blackmore's novel contains a powerful mixture of drama and romance, all told in a very visual manner, so it is not surprising that over the years at least ten films and TV adaptations have been made, all with the title *Lorna Doone*. The following are the best known. The first were two silent movies: that of 1912, directed by Wilfred Noy, starring Dorothy Bellew; and the 1922 film, directed by Maurice Tourneur, starring Madge Bellamy and John Bowers. Reviewers were impressed by the action scenes.

The 1934 talkie directed by Basil Dean, starring Victoria Hopper, John Loder and Margaret Lockwood (as Annie Ridd), although filmed on Exmoor, received a lukewarm reception in the *New York Times*, and the 1951 film directed by Phil Karlson starring Barbara Hale, Richard Greene and Carl Benton Reid, had similarly mixed reviews. A BBC adaptation for TV in 1963 (11 episodes), directed by Mike Barker, was filmed on location and the storyline remained close to the original novel. It starred Bill Travers, Jane Merrow – praised for her portrayal of Lorna – and Andrew Faulds. In 1976 Joan Craft directed a mini-series (in 5 episodes) for the BBC (filmed on Exmoor), staring John Sommerville, Emily Richard, and John Turner.

A British ITV film in 1990, directed by Andrew Grieve, starring Clive Owen, Polly Walker, and Sean Bean, omitted the Monmouth Rebellion, a key element of the novel. Finally, a BBC One TV movie in 2000, directed by Mike Barker, was complimented for its authenticity and good acting. Starring Richard Coyle, Amelia Warner, and Aiden Gillen, it had an excellent supporting cast including Anton Lesser, Peter Vaughan, and Michael Kitchen.

The Lorna Doone Trail

Through words and pictures this books traces the Exmoor adventures of Jan and Lorna and of some of the most important secondary characters, such as Jeremy Stickles and Tom Faggus. Beginning with Jan's sad journey home from school, it follows the hero and heroine to their ideally happy ending. Blackmore's own words are, of course, of prime authority – and are so employed; but we have added our own commentaries, knowing how often the complexities of the plot and Blackmore's heightened treatment of scene and place baffle the explorer. It is only fair to remind ourselves that he was writing a novel, not a guide-book: he was, in his own words, 'shaping this old tale' in which 'the incidents, characters, time and scenery are alike romantic'.

Mere 'identification', then has never been the main purpose since, where much must remain conjectural, dogmatic assertion would have been foolish and misleading. Where positive statements could be made they are not avoided, for lovers of the novel will receive added pleasure from following confidently in Blackmore's footsteps.

Above all, we have tried in this small compass, to choose quotations and illustrations to capture something of the novel's abounding life – thus hoping to draw our readers back to *Lorna Doone* itself.

The Lorna Doone Trail

Blundell's School, Tiverton

My father ... being a great admirer of learning, and well able to write his name, sent me, his only son, to be schooled at Tiverton ... For the chief boast of that ancient town (next to its woollen-staple) is a worthy grammar-school, the largest in the west of England, founded and handsomely endowed in the year 1604, by Master Peter Blundell, of that same place, clothier ...

The school-house stands beside a stream ... called 'Lowman', which ... is wont to flood into a mighty head of waters ... and most of all when its little co-mate, called the 'Taunton brook' ... comes foaming down like a great roan horse ... Then are the grey stone walls of Blundell on every side encompassed ... And in the very front of the gate, just without the archway, where the ground is paved most handsomely, you can see in copy-letters done a great P.B. of white pebbles. Now, it is the custom and the law that when ... the waxing element lips though it be but a single pebble of the founder's letters, it is in the licence of any boy, soever small and undoctrined, to rush into the great school-rooms ... and scream at the top of his voice, 'P.B.'

Then, with a yell, the boys leap up ... toss their caps to the black-beamed roof, and haply the very books after them ... Then the masters look at one another ... With a spirited bang they close their books, and make invitation the one to the other for pipes and foreign cordials, recommending the chance of the time, and the comfort away from cold water. (Chapter I)

According to the novel, John Rudd left Blundell's on 29 November 1673, but Blackmore depicts the school and its customs very much as they were in his own schooldays (1837–1843). Little, probably, had changed between 1604 and the earlier years of the nineteenth century, and Blackmore was very much a product of the old school. Indeed the 'P.B.' tradition was kept up until the early 1950s – and this despite the fact that the P.B. stones had been moved from Old Blundell's and placed outside the gates of the 'new' school which was built (in 1880–1882) on a spacious site about a mile to the east of the original foundation. One of the finest examples of Jacobean 'domestic' architecture in the West Country, Old Blundell's now belongs to the National Trust. Peter Blundell planned on a munificent scale. The Lord Chief Justice of England was his executor and the school was, as Blackmore puts it, a 'chief boast' of Tiverton – then, and for many a year afterwards, a prosperous centre of the wool trade.

Gateway to Blundell's Old School, founded in 1604 with funds bequeathed for the purpose by Peter Blundell.

The impressive building of Blundell's Old School.

Tiverton

We left the town of the two fords, which they say is the meaning of it, very early in the morning, after lying one day to rest, as was demanded by the nags, sore of foot and foundered. For my part, too, I was glad to rest, having aches all over me, and very heavy bruises; and we lodged at the sign of the White Horse Inn, in the street called Gold Street, opposite where the souls are of John and Joan Greenway, set up in gold letters, because we must take the homeward way at cockcrow of the morning. (Chapter III)

Small wonder that John ached all over after his epic fight with Robin Snell (see Chapter II). Fought out on the famous 'Ironing Box' – 'as the triangle of turf is called, where the two causeways coming from the school-porch and the hall-porch meet' – this struggle resulted in victory for the Exmoor boy, whose heart had responded to John Fry's call: 'Never thee knack under, Jan, or never coom naigh Hexmoor no more'.

At this stage of the story, Jan does not know that his father has been murdered. John Fry keeps the truth from him and he wonders whether 'father had sent for me, because he had a good harvest, and the rats were bad in the corn-chamber'.

The White Horse Inn still stands, its front much altered, but its great entrance yet demonstrating how important it was to travellers in coaching and packhorse days. Opposite, the Greenway Almshouses (1529) testify to the pious benevolence of John and Joan Greenway – benefactors also of St Peter's church, Tiverton's chief architectural glory. Both in the church and on the walls of his almshouses, John Greenway inscribed prayers for his soul and enjoined the passer-by to pray with him: 'Pray for the souls of John and Jone'; 'Have grace, ye men, and ever pray For the soul of John and Jone Grenwaye'. As Martin Dunsford (History of Tiverton, 1790) *wrote: 'By some of his inscriptions ... he seems to have been strongly impressed with dread of a future state of Purgatory'.*

Wool and religion, fire and flood, the siege of the Castle by Parliamentary forces in 1645, the uproar of reform, industrial decline, the Heathcoat renaissance, and now 'key settlement and development status' – such is the history of this bustling, friendly West Country town: 'town of the two fords', nurse of John Ridd's youthful years.

White Horse Inn, Gold Street, Tiverton, where John Fry and Jan Ridd lodged.

Greenway Almshouses (1529), Gold Street, Tiverton.

Bampton and the Dulverton Road

From Tiverton town to the town of Oare is a very long and painful road, and in good truth the traveller must make his way, as the saying is; for the way is still unmade, at least, on this side of Dulverton, although there is less danger now than in the time of my schooling; for now a good horse may go there without much cost of leaping; but when I was a boy, the spurs would fail, when needed most, by reason of the slough-cake. It is to the credit of this age, and our advance upon fatherly ways, that now we have laid down rods and faggots, and even stump-oaks here and there, so that a man in good daylight need not sink, if he be quite sober. There is nothing I have striven at more than doing my duty, way-warden over Exmoor. (Chapter III)

In his assumed character of John Ridd, Blackmore refers to 'the town of Oare'; but Oare is, and has always been, a hamlet. 'Township' means settlement or inhabited place. The rest of the description is strictly accurate. Until the development of turnpikes in the late eighteenth century and the Knight family's purchase of the Forest in the early nineteenth century, there were no roads on Exmoor. Wheeled vehicles were rare: sledges ('trackamucks') were in common use. The road from Tiverton to Bampton did not follow the Exe Valley. Until fairly recent times roads always climbed high, out of the wet lands and the woods. (The term 'slough-cake' means muddy ground, difficult for horses.) John Ridd and the faithful, though often cowardly, John Fry, had a choice of two routes that ran almost parallel out of Tiverton and then combined outside the town: Bampton Street leading into what is now Park Road; and Frog Street leading into Long Causeway (now Castle Street and Bartow's Causeway) and ending today at the park. Whichever route they took would have brought them to Knight-shayes – no mansion there in those days – and through the wandering hilly lanes to Bampton. This attractive town was renowned for its centuries-old Charter Fair at which, between 1856 and 1985, Exmoor ponies were sold. The Fair still takes place on the last Thursday in October. A small-scale pony sale was reintroduced just outside Bampton as part of the Fair in 2004; however, this came to an end after about a decade due to lack of demand.

As their first 'baiting-place' was to be Dulverton, Jan and John would have ridden along Brook Street with its stylish architecture, up Fore Street and then taken the narrow High Street (to the right of where the war memorial now stands). This led them, as it leads us, to High Cross – where the ghostly chains rattle on winter nights – and past Combe Head until, at the summit of Grant's Hill, they would see their first Exmoor panorama. Then, a long drop down towards Higher Grant's Farm – nearly out of Devon, but so typically Devonian in its beauty – swinging left at the old toll house (not there in John Ridd's day) onto the B3222 and into charming Exebridge where Devon ends and Somerset begins.

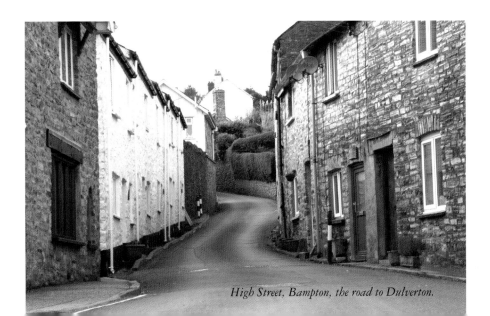

High Street, Bampton, the road to Dulverton.

Brook Street, Bampton.

Exebridge and Tom Faggus

The road from Bampton to Dulverton had not been very delicate, yet nothing to complain of much – no deeper, indeed, than the hocks of a horse. (Chapter III)

For the day-boys [of Blundell's] had brought us word that some [packmen] intending their way to the town [of Tiverton] ... must be in ere nightfall, because Mr Faggus was after them. Now, Mr Faggus was my first cousin, and an honour to the family, being a North Molton man, of great renown on the highway, from Barum [Barnstaple] town even to London. (Chapter II)

Much cause had he to be harsh with the world; and yet all acknowledged him pleasant, when a man gave up his money ... By trade he had been a blacksmith, in the town of North Molton ... a rough rude place at the end of Exmoor ... Not only could he read and write, but he had solid substance; a piece of land worth a hundred pounds, and right of common for two hundred sheep, and a score-and-a-half of beasts ... and made such a fame at the shoeing of horses, that the farriers of Barum were like to lose their custom ... when ... a lawyer's writ fell upon him ... This was the beginning of a law-suit with Sir Robert Bampfylde, a gentleman of the neighbourhood, who tried to oust him from his common, and drove his cattle,

The Old Smithy at North Molton reputed to be where Tom Faggus plied his trade as a blacksmith.

Bridge over the River Exe at Exebridge.

Exebridge. On the right is the inn where Tom Faggus was captured.

and harassed them. And by that suit of law poor Tom was ruined altogether ... and he took it to heart so grievously that he said ... 'The world hath preyed on me, like a wolf. God help me now to prey on the world' ... Everybody cursed the Doones, who lived apart disdainfully. But all good people liked Mr Faggus – when he had not robbed them – and many a poor sick man or woman blessed him for other people's money; and all the hostlers, stableboys and tapsters entirely worshipped him. (Chapter XII)

The road to Dulverton would have been a greater ordeal but for the fine old bridge over the Exe. Here, just below the confluence of the Barle and the Exe rivers, is the vital crossing place – and here has stood for centuries an inn for the refreshment of man and beast.

Tom Faggus – a West Country Robin Hood – plays a large part in the story. He eventually receives a pardon for his highway robberies, marries Jan Ridd's sister Annie and is involved in both the Doone plot and the Monmouth Rebellion. Finally, he reforms. Blackmore did not invent Faggus. According to legend, he was captured in the inn at Exebridge. His famous strawberry mare, Winnie, was shot, and the intrepid highwayman was hanged at Taunton.

Dulverton

It was high noon before we were got to Dulverton that day ... My mother had an uncle living there, but we were not to visit his house this time, at which I was somewhat astonished, since we needs must stop for at least two hours, to bait our horses thorough well, before coming to the black bogway ... But now, at Dulverton, we dined upon the rarest and choicest victuals that ever I did taste. Even now, at my time of life, to think of it gives me appetite, as once and awhile to think of my first love makes me love all goodness. Hot mutton pasty was a thing I had often heard of from wealthy boys and men, who made a dessert of dinner; and to hear them talk of it made my lips smack, and my ribs come inwards.

And now John Fry strode into the hostel, with the air and grace of a short-legged man, and shouted as loud as if he was calling sheep upon Exmoor: 'Hot mootton pasty for twoo trarv'lers, at number vaive, in vaivve minnits! Dish un up in the tin with the grahvy, zame as I hardered last Tuesday.'

Of course it did not come in five minutes, nor yet in ten ... but that made it all the better when it came ... and the smell of it was enough to make an empty man thank God for the room there was inside him. Fifty years have passed me quicker than the taste of that gravy. (Chapter III)

Still unaware that his father is dead, John Ridd smacks his lips over his Dulverton food – as many a traveller has done since his day. We cannot be certain which Dulverton hostelry Blackmore had in mind: there were a score of taverns and hotels in the delectable little town. Today, the Lion and the Bridge are the sole proud survivors of a goodly company, but several more recent restaurants and cafés also provide excellent food and drink. It is at the inn that the boy first encounters the mysterious foreign lady's-maid whose fate is bound up with Lorna's family.

Throughout the novel Blackmore depicts Dulverton as a moorland metropolis, where luxuries may be purchased and where news of the great world abounds. Sheltered in its deep bowl, it drew ample water power from the Barle for its fulling and grist mills. Busy shops – then as now – served the scattered moorland folk; and it was at Dulverton that the roads ended and 'the black bogway' began.

Dulverton today, a busy moorland town as depicted in the novel.

Mr Reuben Huckaback

Mr Reuben Huckaback, whom many good folk in Dulverton will remember long after my time, was my mother's uncle ... He owned the very best shop in the town, and did a fine trade in soft ware, especially when the pack-horses came safely in at Christmas-time ... And truly, the Dulverton people said that he was the richest man in their town, and could buy up half the county armigers; ay, and if it came to that, they would like to see any man, at Bampton, or at Wiveliscombe, and you might say almost Taunton, who could put down golden Jacobus and Carolus against him ... Now it pleased God ... (in spite of all the fogs) to send safe home

to Dulverton, and what was more, with their loads quite safe, a goodly string of pack-horses. Nearly half of their charge was for Uncle Reuben, and he knew how to make the most of it. Then, having balanced his debits and credits, and set writs running against defaulters, as behoves a good Christian at Christmas-tide, he saddled his horse, and rode off towards Oare ... (Chapter XIII)

Jan's Uncle Reuben is a comic character who plays an indirect but important part in the story. Grandfather of Ruth – who loves Jan and saves his life when the doctors are bleeding him to death – he opens a mine near the Wizard's Slough and is thus instrumental in reuniting the mine 'Captain', Simon Carfax, with his daughter, Gwenny, who is Lorna's maid and companion. Reuben Huckaback is also an ingenious conspirator when the downfall of the Doones is being planned. His position as the wealthiest man in Dulverton reinforces Blackmore's insistence on the importance and prosperity of the town.

This photograph of Church Lane brings out the enduring character and charm of the place where Huckaback would have walked to worship in church – or to dun his debtors! Despite modernisation of buildings and ever-increasing traffic, its tall-chimneyed cottages, narrow streets and shy courts, hidden from the careless passerby, still give one a glimpse of the Dulverton that R.D. Blackmore – or, indeed, Jan Ridd – would have recognised.

Before the 1830s, packhorses were the main means of transporting goods on Exmoor. In the words of Hope Bourne in Living on Exmoor, *'merchandise from the townships, produce to market, lime from the kiln, manure to the fields, corn to the barn. Summer and winter, in all weathers, the ponies splashed through the fords and rattled over the little bridges, nine in a string, their packs swaying and bells ringing, on their way from farm to farm and to the outer world.'*

    An 'armiger' was someone entitled to bear heraldic arms. Golden 'Jacobus' and 'Carolus' were gold coins struck in the reigns of James I and Charles I.

Opposite: *A typical string of packhorses crossing a narrow packhorse bridge. Many such medieval bridges can still be seen on Exmoor.* (© Elizabeth Robinson)

Church Lane, Dulverton.

Chibbet Post

The fog came down upon the moors as thick as ever I saw it; and there was no sound of any sort, nor a breath of wind to guide us ... John Fry was bowing forward with sleep upon his saddle ...

'Mercy of God! Where be us now?' said John Fry, waking suddenly; 'us ought to have passed hold hash, Jan. Zeen it on the road have 'ee?'

'No indeed, John; no old ash. Nor nothing else to my knowing; nor heard nothing, save thee snoring.'

'Watt a vule thee must be then, Jan; and me myzell no better. Harken lad, harken!'

We drew our horses up and listened, through the thickness of the air, and with our hands laid to our ears ... Then there came a mellow noise, very low and

An engraving of a gibbet from the 1886 edition of Lorna Doone. *This conveys the macabre atmosphere of the scene eloquently described by Blackmore.*

mournsome, not a sound to be afraid of, but to long to know the meaning, with a soft rise of the hair. Three times it came and went again ... and then I touched John Fry to know that there was something near me ...

'Have they hanged one of the Doones then, John?'

'Hush, lad; never talk laike o' thiccy. Hang a Doone! God knoweth the King would hang pretty quick, if her did.'

'Then who is it in chains, John?' ...

'It be nawbody,' said John, 'vor us to make a fush about. Belong to t'other zide o' the moor, and come staling shape to our zide. Red Jem Hannaford his name. Thank God for him to be hanged, lad; and good cess to his soul for craiken' zo.'

So the sound of the quiet swinging led us ... even as far as the foot of the gibbet where the four cross-ways are ...

I was sorry for Red Jem ... But John would talk no more about it ... 'Hould thee tongue, lad,' he said sharply; 'us be naigh the Doone-track

Chibbet Post today.

now, two maile from Dunkery Beacon hill ... so happen they be abroad tonight, us must crawl on our belly-places, boy.' (Chapter III)

Although Chibbet (Gibbet) Post (south west of Exford) is more than 3 miles from Dunkery Beacon, that is almost certainly the place where Red Jem was hanging and providing such a useful landmark for benighted travellers. John and Jan are well clear of Dulverton now and heading for Plover's Barrows. Even as the crow flies, they still have about 7 moorland miles – and the perils of the Doones – ahead.

Dunkery Beacon

I heard something, and caught John's arm ... It was the sound of horses' feet, knocking up through splashy ground ... Then a grunting of weary men, and the lifting noise of stirrups ...

'Let goo braidle; let goo, lad. Plaise God they take them for forest-ponies, or they'll zend a bullet through us.' I saw what he meant and let go the bridle, for now the mist was rolling off, and we were against the sky-line to the dark cavalcade below us ... then just as the foremost horseman passed, scarce twenty yards below us, a puff of wind came up the glen, and the fog rolled off before it. And suddenly a strong red light, cast by the cloud-weight downwards, spread like fingers over the moorland, opened the alleys of darkness, and hung on the steel of the riders.

'Dunkery Beacon,' whispered John ... the beacon was rushing up, in a fiery storm to heaven, and the form of its flame came and went in the folds, and the heavy sky was hovering ... a giant beard of fire streamed throughout the darkness. The sullen hills were flanked with light, and the valleys chined with shadow ...

the flinging fire leaped into the rocky mouth of the glen below me, where the horsemen passed in silence, scarcely deigning to look round. Heavy men, and large of stature, reckless how they bore their guns, or how they sat their horses, with leathern jerkins, and long boots, and iron plates on breast and head, plunder heaped behind their saddles ... Some had carcasses of sheep swinging with their skins on, others had deer, and one had a child flung across his saddle-bow. Whether the child were dead, or alive, was beyond my vision. (Chapter III)

At 1705 feet (519 m) Dunkery Hill is the highest point on Exmoor. When the weather is clear, the views all round are magnificent. On the shoulders of the hill lie the remains of Bronze Age burial cairns. At the very top, one of these formed the base of a beacon, which, from the fourteenth to the seventeenth century, was part of a network of hilltop warning signals ready to be lit when invasion threatened. In the novel, the Doones have appropriated it (by the brutal expedient of throwing the watchman onto the fire). In this grimly dramatic scene, it is lighting their way home after a raid that has far-reaching consequences for both Jan and Lorna.

Dunkery Beacon from the north showing the wild nature of the moor. The beacon is on the central hill.

View from heather-clad Dunkery Beacon looking towards the Bristol Channel.   (© Paul Savage)

Death on the Road from Porlock

My dear father had been killed by the Doones of Badgworthy, while riding home from Porlock market ... With him were six brother-farmers, all of them very sober; for father would have no company with any man who went beyond half-a-gallon of beer, or a single gallon of cider.... [They] were jogging along, helping one another in the troubles of the road, and singing goodly hymns and songs, to keep their courage moving, when suddenly a horseman stopped in the starlight full across them.

By dress and arms they knew him well, and by his size and stature, shown against the glimmer of the evening star; and though he seemed one man to seven, it was in truth one man to one. Of the six who had been singing songs and psalms ... there was not one but pulled out his money, and sang small beer to a Doone.

But my father ... set his staff above his head, and rode at the Doone robber. With a trick of his horse, the wild man escaped the sudden onset ... Then, when Smiler [Ridd's horse] was carried away with the dash and weight of my father ... the outlaw ... plundered the rest of the yeomen. But father, drawing at Smiler's head, to try to come back and help them, was in the midst of a dozen men, who seemed to come out of a turf-rick, some on horse, some a-foot. Nevertheless, he smote lustily, so far as he could see, and being of great size and strength, and his blood well up, they had no easy job with him ... But a man beyond the range of staff was crouching by the peat-stack, with a long gun set to his shoulder, and he got poor father against the sky, and I cannot tell the rest of it. Only they knew that Smiler came home, with blood upon his withers, and father was found in the morning dead on the moor. (Chap. IV)

Blackmore gives no precise location for this dreadful attack on the elder John Ridd. It might have occurred on Porlock Common or, as some would have it, near Robber's Bridge down in the Oare valley.

Peat turves were used as domestic fuel into the twentieth century. The turves were cut in the spring and left to dry. Then they were built into high ricks or stacks until needed for the fire.

Robber's Bridge. In the past, the country around this packhorse bridge, on a minor road from Porlock Hill, was a place where bandits lurked.

Lorna Doone Farm at Malmsmead. This house dates from the late sixteenth or early seventeenth century.

Location of Plover's Barrows Farm

Oftentimes I looked at his gun, an ancient piece found in the sea ... and it hurt me to see how John handled it, as if he had no memory. 'Bad job for he, as her had not got thiccy, the naught as her coom across them Doones ... a maight have been gooin' to market now, 'stead of laying banked up, over yanner. Maister Jan, thee can zee the grave if thee look alang this here goonbarryel ...' (Chapter VI)

Almost everybody knows ... how pleasant and soft the fall of the land is round about Plover's Barrows Farm. All above it is strong dark mountain, spread with heath and desolate, but near our house the valleys cove, and open warmth and shelter. Here are ... orchards full of contentment, and a man may scarce espy the brook although he hears it everywhere. And indeed a stout good piece of it comes through our farm-yard and swells sometimes to a rush of waves when the clouds are on the hill-tops ... But about two miles below our farm, the Badgworthy Water runs into the Lyn and makes a real river of it. (Chapter VII)

The popularity of Lorna Doone *has stimulated numerous pamphlets that have sought to prove that Plover's Barrows Farm was here or that the Doone Valley was there. It is a waste of time to attempt this kind of identification. Blackmore knew that his novel was a romance and he would have laughed himself silly at the efforts of self-styled 'researchers' to pin him down. The topographical 'interpretations' of* Lorna Doone *cancel each other out if the reader*

Bridge at Malmsmead in the spring.

48

Oareford Farm beyond the ford across Oare Water. This house vies with Lorna Doone Farm as a possible model for Plover's Barrows.

brings a grain of commonsense – and the evidence of the Ordnance Survey Map – to bear on the blinkered interpretations of fanatics who have stridently argued their so-called cases.

'Farmer Snow came up to Plover's Barrows'. Well, he could have done so just as plausibly if he had lived at the present Lorna Doone Farm and the Ridds had lived at Oareford Farm or if their respective conjectural domiciles had been interchanged. This is merely one example of the kind of useless 'trump-card' that the protagonists use in their arguments.

We can get no sense out of these sterile debates. Better, simply, to enjoy the book – recognize that Blackmore based the novel on his memories of 'Doone Country'. Unless we are sensible we shall litter the Exmoor landscape with as many debatable 'Plover's Barrows Farms' and 'water slides' as there were fragments of 'the true cross' in medieval Europe.

Porlock

In very quick time, I ran away with the shilling in my pocket, and got Peggy out on the Porlock road, without my mother knowing it. For mother was frightened of that road now, as if all the trees were murderers ... And, to tell the truth, I was touched with fear for many years about it; and even now, when I ride at dark there, a man by a peat rick makes me shiver, until I go and collar him. But this time I was very bold, having John Fry's blunderbuss, and keeping a sharp look-out wherever any lurking-place was. However, I saw only sheep, and small red cattle, and the common deer of the forest, until I was near to Porlock town, and then rode straight to Mr Pooke's, at the sign of the Spit and Gridiron.

Mr Pooke was asleep, as it happened, not having much to do that day ... and in I walked with a manful style, bearing John Fry's blunderbuss. Now Timothy Pooke was a peaceful man, glad to live without any enjoyment of mind at danger, and I was tall and large already, as most lads of a riper age. Mr Pooke, as soon as he opened his eyes, dropped suddenly under the counter-board and drew a great frying-pan over his head, as if the Doones were come to rob him ...

The Ship Inn, Porlock, one of Tom Faggus's haunts. Of sixteenth- or seventeenth-century origin, this inn has been much altered over the centuries.

The sea at Porlock Weir.

'Gadzooks, Master Pooke,' said I, having learned fine words at Tiverton, 'do you suppose that I know not then the way to carry firearms?'

... 'God sake, John Ridd, God sake, dear boy,' cried Pooke, knowing me by this time: 'don't 'ee, for good love now, don't 'ee show it to me, boy, as if I were to suck it. Put 'un down, for good, now; and thee shall have the very best of all is in the shop.' ...

But in spite of all assurances, he showed himself desirous only to see the last of my gun and me ... For my shilling Master Pooke afforded me two great packages [of gunpowder] ... as well as a mighty chunk of lead ... And as if all this had not been enough, he presented me with a roll of comfits for my sister Annie, whose gentle face and pretty manners won the love of everybody. (Chapter VI)

John's journey takes him along the fatal road where his father was murdered. Practice with his father's long gun fits him for the battle with the Doones that must come.

Porlock was a busy market town catering for the needs of north Exmoor folk. It is here that, later in the novel, John visits a 'middling honest lawyer' to draw up his will. Surrounded by truly fertile land and linked with Porlock Weir – through which so many goods were imported (some paid Excise Duty; many did not) – it was conscious of its own importance. The Ship Inn, at the foot of Porlock Hill, was the scene of one of Tom Faggus's exploits.

Porlock Weir, a port of some importance in the seventeenth century for both legal imports and smuggling.

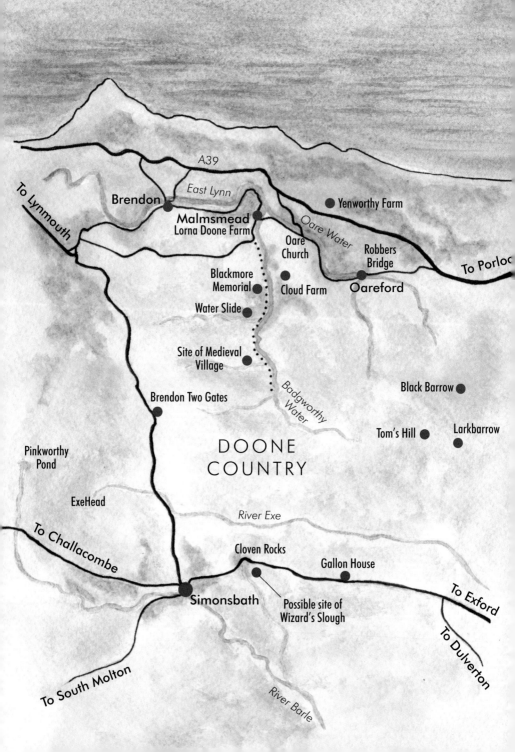

A39

To Lynmouth

East Lynn

Brendon

Malmsmead
Lorna Doone Farm

Yenworthy Farm

Oare Water

Oare
Church

Robbers
Bridge

To Porloc

Blackmore
Memorial

Cloud Farm

Oareford

Water Slide

Site of Medieval
Village

Badgworthy
Water

Black Barrow

Brendon Two Gates

Tom's Hill

Larkbarrow

Pinkworthy
Pond

DOONE
COUNTRY

ExeHead

River Exe

To Challacombe

Cloven Rocks

Gallon House

To Exford

Simonsbath

Possible site of
Wizard's Slough

To Dulverton

To South Molton

River Barle

Badgworthy Water

Thence [the Lyn river] hurries away, with strength and a force of wilful waters, under the foot of a bare-faced hill, and so to rocks and woods again, where the stream is covered over, and dark, heavy pools delay it. There are plenty of fish all down this way, and the further you go the bigger they be, having deeper grounds to feed in ... yet it so happened that neither [my sister Annie nor I] had been up the Badgworthy Water ... For Badgworthy Water ran out of Doone Valley, a mile or so from the mouth of it. But when I was turned fourteen years old ... it happened to me without choice, I may say, to explore the Badgworthy Water ... to get some loaches for [my mother] ...

When I had travelled two miles or so ... suddenly, in an open space, where meadows spread about it, I found a good stream flowing softly into the body of our brook. And it brought, so far as I could guess by the sweep of it under my kneecaps, a larger power of clear water than the Lyn itself had; only it came more quietly down, not being troubled with stairs and steps as the fortune of the Lyn is, but gliding smoothly and forcibly, as if upon some set purpose. Hereupon I drew up, and thought ... it was a frightful thing ... to venture, where no grown

Badgworthy Water. Its tranquillity belies the drama of the novel.

man durst, up the Badgworthy Water ... However ... my spirit arose within me ... and crossing the Lyn [I] went stoutly up under the branches which hang so dark on the Badgworthy river. (Chapter VII)

The romantic aspects of Blackmore's descriptions of 'Doone Land' scenery are illustrated by these extracts. The first paragraph purports to be a description of the East Lyn, but is couched in such general terms that it could apply to any one of a dozen Exmoor rivers in their lower courses. Then comes the ominous mention of Badgworthy Water which neither Annie nor Jan has explored, because 'Badgworthy Water ran out of Doone Valley'. That statement alone should have put paid to the amateur detective work of the 'Doone Valley sleuths'. Nothing on the ground supports Blackmore's imagined relationship between Badgworthy and the various tributary combes that feed it.

From the junction between Hoccombe Water and Long Combe where, under the molinia-clad ridge of Trout Hill, these two moorland valleys meet and turn due north to form Badgworthy, the lovely stream deepens until it adds its waters to the East Lyn. Badgworthy does not run out *of anything: several small tributaries enter it before it joins Oare Water and then becomes the East Lyn. Blackmore's description gives a heightened idea of Badgworthy's power; though its beauty cannot be exaggerated. Again – see the Introduction – one should remember that he was writing a novel, not a guide-book.*

The Doone Valley with Badgworthy Water running through it.

The Doones' Settlement

For she stood at the head of a deep green valley, carved from out the mountains in a perfect oval, with a fence of sheer rock standing round it, eighty feet or a hundred high; from whose brink black wooded hills swept up to the sky line. By her side a little river glided out ... lapsed away, and fell into the valley ... further down, on either bank, were covered houses, built of stone, square and roughly cornered, set as if the brook were meant to be the street between them. Only one room high they were, and not placed opposite each other, but in and out as skittles are; only that the first of all, which proved to be the captain's, was a sort of double house, or rather two houses joined together by a plank-bridge over the river.

Fourteen cots my mother counted, all very much of a pattern ... Deep in the quiet valley there, away from noise, and violence, and brawl, save that of the rivulet, any man would have deemed them homes of simple mind and innocence. Yet not a single house stood there but was the home of murder. (Chapter IV)

The above description of the outlaws' stronghold tallies with those given later in the book, though the water slide and Doone Gate are added as dramatic features in further episodes.

This photograph shows the area of the medieval settlement where Blackmore placed the Doone village at the eastern end of Hoccombe Combe. Grass-covered mounds are all that can now be seen of the ancient houses. (© Exmoor National Park Authority).

The most important words in Blackmore's first account of the dreaded valley make the ironical statement that 'any man would have deemed them {the Doone houses} homes of simple mind and innocence'. This proves that he was describing the ancient Badgworthy settlement, occupied for centuries by hermits and holy men. When the Doones settled in the uninhabited Royal Forest of Exmoor the only houses available to them were those that had formed this deserted medieval village. Alfred Vowles (see Reading List) traced fourteen ruined houses when he investigated the valley. We must recognise, however, that the ravages of Exmoor weather have destroyed much that was visible to him. Today, a few mounds give little idea of the ground plan that Blackmore knew and that Vowles reconstructed at the eastern extremity of Hoccombe Combe.

The natural features were dramatised by Blackmore. There are no mountains. The Doone Gate is imaginary. The water slide (see p.58) is not fearsome. A dozen different Exmoor scenes were fused to produce 'Doone Land'. Even so, the imaginative reader will always see Badgworthy through Blackmore's eyes.

The water slide in Lank Combe that may have given Blackmore the idea for the much more impressive one described in the novel.

The Water Slide

And so, in a sorry plight, I came to an opening in the bushes, where a great black pool lay in front of me ... And the look of this black pit was enough to stop one from diving into it, even on a hot summer's day with sunshine on the water; I mean, if the sun ever shone there ... But soon I saw the reason for the stir and depth of that great pit, as well as of the roaring sound which long had made me wonder ... For, lo! I stood at the foot of a long pale slide of water, coming smoothly to me, without any break or hindrance, for a hundred yards or more, and fenced on either side with cliff, sheer, and straight, and shining. The water neither ran nor fell, nor leaped with any spouting, but made one even slope of it, as if it had been combed or planed, and looking like a plank of deal laid down a deep black staircase. (Chapter VII)

Fishing for loaches in Badgworthy Water, Jan suddenly and terrifyingly comes upon the water slide. With great courage (and great fear) the boy fights his way up this huge barrier and, nearly drowning, penetrates the Doone Valley, where he has his first meeting with Lorna.

Controversy rages about the precise identification of the water slide. Ingenuity is strained to 'prove' that this or that combe is its original. There is little doubt that Blackmore knew Lank Combe where – on a pigmy scale compared with the description in the novel – the water does, indeed, come gliding down the rocks 'in a long pale slide'. It would be perverse to argue that Lank Combe was not the germ of the water slide. We must, however, keep a sense of proportion. Blackmore legitimately combined and exaggerated natural features to provide

an epic background for his stirring narrative. Just as the present Lorna Doone Farm, and other old buildings round about, suggested material for Plover's Barrows, so Badgworthy, Hoccombe Combe and Lank Combe gave him the basis for his magnificent description of the Doone Valley. Blackmore does not consistently indicate that his imaginary Doone Valley was a tributary opening into Badgworthy. Had he done so, there would be some point in getting steamed up about the rival claims of Hoccombe Combe and Lank Combe.

As it is, let us be thankful that all this superb 'Doone Land' is readily accessible from Malmsmead: and let us use our imagination – as Blackmore used his.

The rocks below the water slide may have inspired Blackmore's description of the dramatic 'cliffs' on either side.

Lee Abbey, formerly Ley (or Lee) Manor. The present buildings date from the 1850s and little remains of the seventeenth-century manor house where the Wichehalse family lived.

(Pete Rae © Exmoor National Park Authority).

Robbery on the Moor

I ... presently was met, point-blank, by the head of a mountain-pony. Upon its back lay a man, bound down, with his feet on the neck and his head to the tail, and his arms falling down like stirrups. The wild little nag was scared of its life by the unaccustomed burden, and had been tossing and rolling hard, in desire to get ease of it ...

Of course, the Doones and nobody else, had robbed good Uncle Reuben; ... and took his horse, an especially sober nag, and bound the master upon the wild one ... For two or three hours they had fine enjoyment, chasing him through the fog, and making much sport of his groanings; and then waxing hungry they went their way, and left him to opportunity. (Chapter XIII)

Determined to get a warrant against the Doones, Huckaback visits the Devon J.P., Baron De Whichehalse, at Ley Manor (now Lee Abbey). But he is subtly mocked and sent on his way without receiving any support.

All throughout the homeward road, Uncle Ben had been very silent, feeling much displeased ... But before he went to bed that night, he just said to me, '... Now, mark my words, this villain job shall not have ending here. I have another card to play.'

'You mean, sir, I suppose, that you will go to the justices of this county; Squire Maunder, or Sir Richard Blewitt, or –'

'Oaf, I mean nothing of the sort; they would only make a laughing-stock, as those Devonshire people did, of me. No, I will go to the King himself, or a man who is bigger than the King, and to whom I have ready access. I will not tell thee his name at present; only if thou art brought before him, never wilt thou forget it.' That was true enough, by the by, as I discovered afterwards; for the man he meant was Judge Jeffreys. (Chapter XV)

Huckaback does indeed demand justice of Judge Jeffreys and, as a result, Jan finds himself ordered to appear as a witness before the Court of King's Bench in London. There he meets the fearsome judge.

The High Moor

It was a long flat sweep of moorland over which he was gazing, with a few bogs here and there, and brushy places round them. Of course, John Fry, from his shepherd life, and reclaiming of strayed cattle, knew as well as need be where he was, and the spread of the hills before him, although it was beyond our beat ... but he liked it none the more for that, neither did any of our people; and, indeed, all the neighbourhood of Thomshill and Larksborough, and most of all Black Barrow Down, lay under the grave imputation of having been enchanted with a very evil spell. Moreover, it was known, though folk were loath to speak of it, even on a summer morning, that Squire Thom, who had been murdered there, a century ago or more, had been seen by several shepherds, even in the middle day, walking with his severed head carried in his left hand, and his right arm lifted towards the sun. Therefore it was very bold in John ... to venture across that moor alone ... For, carefully spying across the moor, from behind the tuft of whortles, at first he could discover nothing having life and motion, except three or four wild cattle roving in vain search for nourishment and a diseased sheep banished hither, and some carrion crows keeping watch on her. (Chapter XXXI)

In this incident John Fry is tracking Reuben Huckaback, whose mysterious journeys into the wild moorland have excited the curiosity of the Ridds. The wily old merchant is, in fact, prospecting for the mineral wealth which he hopes to add to his already considerable store.

The passage is a good example of Blackmore's skill in evoking the Exmoor scene. The Doone Country (illustrated in pictures and words on pp. 54-59) is surrounded by a high plateau where rolling moor lines, golden molinia grass, flying cloud shadows, lark song and curlew call (the latter sadly increasingly rare) exhilarate the traveller on a sunny day – in striking contrast to the eerie shapes and the stark desolation that threaten him when the mists fall or when dusk begins. Then, indeed, he quickens his steps as best he may, to be off the moor before night and its spectres overtake him.

The illustration overleaf shows John Knight's Forest Wall. To the north of the wall (on its left in the photograph) is Brendon Common: south lies the Forest. Hoccombe Water sweeps down from Brendon Two Gates to its junction with Long Combe. The cleft of Badgworthy runs from right to left, while on the skyline Black Barrow Down and the upper reaches of Long Combe can be seen.

Doone country. John Knight's Forest Wall on the right near Brendon Two Gates looking east.

The Valley of Rocks

Now the wisest person in all our parts was reckoned to be a certain wise woman, well known all over Exmoor by the name of 'Mother Melldrum' ... [She] had two homes ... according to the time of year. In summer she lived in a pleasant cave, facing the cool side of the hill, far inland near Hawkridge, and close above 'Tarr Steps', a wonderful crossing of the Barle river, made (as everybody knows) by Satan, for a wager. But throughout the winter, she found sea-air agreeable, and a place where things could be had on credit, and more occasion of talking. Not but what she could have credit (for every one was afraid of her) in the neighbourhood of Tarr Steps; only there was no one handy owning things worth taking.

Therefore, at the fall of the leaf, when the woods grew damp and irksome, the wise woman always set her face to the warmer cliffs of the Channel; where shelter was, and dry fern bedding, and folk to be seen ... And there ... anyone who chose

Tarr Steps, a clapper bridge, probably of medieval origin.

Feral goats in the Valley of Rocks.

might find her, towards the close of a winter's day, gathering sticks and brown fern for fuel, and talking to herself the while, in a hollow stretch behind the cliffs; which foreigners who come and go without seeing much of Exmoor have called the 'Valley of Rocks'.

This valley, or 'goyal' [goyle], as we term it ... lies to the west of Lynton ... Our homefolk always call it the 'Danes', or the 'Denes'; which is no more, they tell me, than a hollow place ... It is a green rough-sided hollow, bending at the middle, touched with stone at either crest, and dotted here and there with slabs, in and out the brambles. On the right hand is an upward crag, called by some the 'Castle', easy enough to scale, and giving great view of the Channel. Facing this, from the inland side and the elbow of the valley, a queer old pile of rock arises, bold behind one another, and quite enough to affright a man ... This is called the 'Devil's Cheese-ring' or the 'Devil's Cheese-knife', which mean the same thing, as our fathers were used to eat their cheese from a scoop; and perhaps in old time the upmost rock ... was like to such an implement if Satan eat cheese untoasted ....

Now Mother Melldrum kept her winter in this vale of rocks, sheltering from the wind and rain within the Devil's Cheese-ring; which added greatly to her fame,

The Valley of Rocks.

because all else, for miles around, were afraid to go near it after dark, or even on a gloomy day. (Chapter XVII)

John Ridd, however, has the courage to consult Mother Melldrum about his love for Lorna Doone. His interview with the wise woman is terminated by defiance on his part and oracular words from her. Then comes the famous fight between the 'fine fat sheep' and the 'lean black goat'. The Valley of Rocks is a dry valley, once the course of the two Lyn rivers, and now weathered and eroded into fantastic shapes.

Gallon House

While John [Fry] was trembling within himself ... to his great amazement something white arose out of the hole, under the brown trunk of the tree. Seeing this his blood went back within him; yet he was not able to turn and flee, but rooted his face in among the loose stones, and kept his quivering shoulders back, and prayed to God to protect him. However, the white thing itself was not so very awful, being nothing more than a long-coned night-cap with a tassel on the top, such as criminals wear at hanging-time. But when John saw a man's face under it, and a man's neck and shoulders slowing rising out of the pit, he could not doubt that this was the place where the murderers come to life again, according to the Exmoor story. He knew that a man had been hanged last week, and that this was the ninth day after it.

Therefore he could bear no more ... neither did he wait to see what became of the gallows-man; but climbed on his horse with what speed he might, and rode away at full gallop. Neither did he dare go back the way he came, fearing to face Black Barrow Down. Therefore he struck up the other track leading away towards Cloven Rocks, and after riding hard for an hour and drinking all his whisky, he luckily fell in with a shepherd, who led him on to a public-house somewhere near Exford. And here he was so unmanned, the excitement being over, that nothing less than a gallon of ale and half a gammon of bacon, brought him to his right mind again. And he took good care to be home before dark, having followed a well-known sheep-track. (Chapter XXXI)

Gallon House, between Exford and Simonsbath, the pub where John Fry consumed 'a gallon of ale and half a gammon of bacon'.

John Fry's stalking of Reuben Huckaback (see page 63) culminates in this alarming incident. In fact, John has unwittingly stumbled on the secret of Reuben's mine which, as we have seen (page 36), plays an important part in the plot. The blend of tension, humour, local legend and vivid description is typical of Blackmore at his best.

Topographically, the material is of great interest: 'a public house somewhere near Exford' (where John Fry consumes such modest quantities of beer and bacon!) may be confidently identified as Gallon House – once known as Red Deer. However, the wording 'somewhere near Exford' should put us on our guard against dogmatic pin-pointings: Gallon House (no longer a pub) is almost exactly half-way between Exford and Simonsbath. Cloven Rocks and Black Barrow are real places and Blackmore sites them accurately. Yet he leaves romantically and conveniently vague the precise spatial relationship between those two key points, Plover's Barrows and the Wizard's Slough.

Landacre Bridge

It appears that as he [Jeremy Stickles] was riding towards us, from the town of South Molton in Devonshire, he found the roads very soft and heavy, and the floods out in all directions; but met with no other difficulty until he came to Landacre Bridge. He had only a single trooper with him, a man ... whom Jeremy had brought from Exeter. As these two descended towards the bridge, they observed that both the Kensford Water and the River Barle were pouring down in mighty floods ... only the parapets of the bridge could be seen above the water ... On the crown of the bridge [Jeremy] turned his horse to watch the trooper's passage, and to help him with directions; when suddenly he saw him fall headlong into the torrent, and heard the report of a gun from behind, and felt a shock to his own body, such as lifted him out of the saddle. Turning round he beheld three man, risen up from behind the hedge on one side of his onward road ... he struck the spurs into the nag and rode through the water straight at the man who was pointing the long gun at him ... luckily the horse galloped right on without any need for swimming ... 'If they do not catch me up, or shoot me, in the course of the first two miles, I may see my home again,' this was what he said to himself, as he turned to mark what they were about, from the brow of the steep hill. He saw the flooded valley shining with the breadth of water, and the trooper's horse on the other side ... and half-way down the hill he saw the three Doones mounting hastily. And then he knew that his only chance lay in the stoutness of his steed. (Chapter XLVII)

Jeremy Stickles, King's Messenger, plays an important part in the novel. His job is to investigate the anti-papist movements that led so many men from the Exmoor area to the fatal field of Sedgemoor and to the Bloody Assizes. He also keeps a sharp eye on the Doones; and the Doones are out to get him.

The whole of Chapter XLVII repays most careful reading – sadly, space does not permit extended quotation. However, if The Lorna Doone Trail sends its readers back to Blackmore, it will have done its work.

Gripping as a narrative, the chapter throws light on Blackmore's handling of place and scene. Precision of location and deliberate vagueness are both employed. (Kentsford Water, by the way, is 'Kinsford', the upper course of Sherdon.) Landacre Bridge is a well-known and beautiful Exmoor feature. The old Swainmote Court used to be held here. 'Landacre – Withycombe – Newland – the Exe': spot on! Jeremy's route can be plotted. 'Passed towards Lucott Hill – struck upon the founts of Lyn – arrived at Plover's Barrows': general direction clear enough, but all detail omitted.

The ancient packhorse bridge that crosses the Barle at Landacre. On the left is the road along which Jeremy Stickles would have made his escape from the Doones.

South Molton

For he loved a maid of South Molton (a currier's daughter I think she was, and her name was Betsy Paramore), and her father had given consent [to their marriage]; and Tom Faggus, wishing to look his best, and be clean of course, had a tailor at work upstairs for him, who had come all the way from Exeter. And Betsy's things were ready too ... when suddenly ... a lawyer's writ fell upon him ...

This was the beginning of a law-suit with Sir Robert Bamfylde ... [who] could pay for much swearing; and then all [Tom's] goods and his farm were sold up, and even his smithery taken. But he saddled his horse, before they could catch him, and rode away to South Molton ... But when he arrived there, instead of comfort, they showed him the face of the door alone; for the news of his

The George Hotel, South Molton, originally a seventeenth-century inn.

loss was before him, and Master Paramore was a sound prudent man, and a high member of the town-council. It is said that they even gave him notice to pay for Betsy's wedding-clothes, now that he was too poor to marry her. This may be false, and indeed I doubt it; in the first place, because South Molton is a busy place for talking; and in the next, that I do not think the action would have lain at law, especially as the maid lost nothing, but used it all for her wedding next month with Dick Vellacott. (Chapter XII)

'And how was it you were struck by a bullet, and only shaken in your saddle? Had you a coat of mail on, or of Milanese chain-armour? Now, Master Stickles, had you?'

'No, Mistress Lizzie; we do not wear things of that kind nowadays. You are apt, I perceive, at romances. But I happened to have a little flat bottle of the very best stoneware slung beneath my saddle-cloak, and filled with the very best *eau de vie* from the George Hotel, at South Molton. The brand of it now is upon my back. Oh, the murderous scoundrels, what a brave spirit they have spilled!' (Chapter XLVII)

So often, the 'yellow' roads on our maps were the chief routes of times past – times when many of our present trunk and main roads did not exist. The South Molton – North Molton – Sandyway – Withypool – Winsford route was an Exmoor lifeline: a reason for the part that this delightful Devonshire town plays in the novel. No reader of Lorna Doone *can leave South Molton unvisited. Local government reorganisation may have dimmed its civic dignity, but the George – praise be! – flourishes. The Guildhall is lovely yet. The Market House, Medical Hall, St Mary Magdalene and the Town Museum offer hours of interest. 'A busy place for talking', says John Ridd – certainly a place to be talked about.*

The centre of South Molton with the Guildhall on the left.

Dunster

West Street, Dunster. (© Paul Savage)

By dinner-time we [Jeremy Stickles and John Ridd] arrived at Porlock, and dined with my old friend, Master Pooke, now growing rich and portly. For though we had plenty of victuals with us, we were not to begin upon them, until all chance of victualling among our friends was left behind. And during that first day we had no need to meddle with our store at all; for as had been settled before we left home, we lay that night at Dunster, in the house of a worthy tanner, first cousin to my mother, who received us very cordially, and undertook to return old Smiler to his stable at Plover's Barrows, after one day's rest.

Thence we hired to Bridgwater; and from Bridgwater on to Bristowe [Bristol], breaking the journey between the two ... And when I let it be known, by some hap, that I was the own cousin of Tom Faggus, and honoured with his society, there was not a house on the road but was proud to entertain me, in spite of my fellow-traveller bearing the red badge of the King.

'I will keep this close, my son Jack,' he said, having stripped it off with a carving-knife; 'your flag is the best to fly.' ...

Therefore we pursued our way, in excellent condition, having thriven upon the credit of that very popular highwayman, and being surrounded with regrets that he had left the profession ...

It was a long and weary journey, although the roads are wondrous good on the further side of Bristowe, and scarcely any man need be bogged, if he keeps his eyes well open, save, perhaps, in Berkshire. (Chapter XXIV)

Escorted by Jeremy Stickles, John Ridd is on his way to London to 'appear in person before the Right Worshipful the Justices of His Majesty's Bench at Westminster ... there to deliver such evidence as is within thy cognizance, touching certain matters whereby the peace of our said lord the King ... is ... impeached, impugned, imperilled, or otherwise detrimented' (see Chapter XXIII). The passage throws an interesting light on the discomforts and perils of seventeenth-century travel and, of course, builds up the fame of Tom Faggus. It also accurately outlines the West Country route to London.

We cannot know which Dunster house Blackmore envisaged as the home of Mrs Ridd's cousin, but the town abounds in old and beautiful buildings.

Thatched cottages at Dunster. (© Paul Savage)

Dunster Castle from the east. (© Paul Savage)

Return to Dunster

It was the beginning of wheat-harvest, when I came to Dunster town, having walked all the way from London, and being somewhat footsore. For though five pounds was enough to keep me in food and lodging upon the road ... it would have been nothing for horse-hire, as I knew too well by the prices Jeremy Stickles had paid, upon our way to London. Now I never saw a prettier town than Dunster looked that evening; for sooth to say, I had almost lost all hope of reaching it that night, although the castle was long in view. But being once there my troubles were gone, at least as regarded wayfaring; for mother's cousin ... was in such indignation at the plight in which I came to him, afoot, and weary, and almost shoeless ... that he swore then, by the mercy of God, that if the schemes abrewing round him, against those bloody Papists, should come to any shape, and show good chance of succeeding, he would risk a thousand pounds, as though it were a penny.

... I think I made him know that the bad state in which I came to his town, and the great shame I had wrought for him among the folk round the card-table at the Luttrell Arms was not to be, even there, attributed to King Charles the Second, nor even to his counsellors, but to my own speed of travelling, which had beat post-horses. For being much distraught in mind, and desperate in body, I had made all the way from London to Dunster in six days, and no more. It may be one hundred and seventy miles, I cannot tell to a furlong or two, especially as I had lost my way more than a dozen times; but at any rate there in six days I was, and most kindly they received me. (Chapter XXVII)

During his first visit to London John Ridd suffers much from 'the law's delay'. He is not called before the Justices and he receives no payment towards his living expenses. A smooth

rogue of a lawyer called Spanks pockets John's allowance and attempts to extort fees from him. John's transparent honesty and outspokenness bring him favourable treatment from Judge Jeffreys when, at last, a lucky chance puts him in that terrifying man's way. Spank is discomfited and offers John reparation. His contempt for the upright yeoman knows no bounds when he refuses to take a penny more than his out-of-pocket expenses. (Hence the mere five pounds with which John set out on the long journey home.)

The Yarn Market, Dunster, with the porch to the Luttrell Arms on the left. (© Paul Savage)

Home to Plover's Barrows

But how shall I tell you the things I felt, and the swelling of my heart within me, as I drew nearer, and more near, to the place of all I loved and owned, to the haunt of every warm remembrance, the nest of all the fledgeling hopes – in a word, to home? The first sheep I beheld on the moor with a great red J.R. on his side ... I do assure you my spirit leaped, and all my sight came to my eyes. I shouted out, 'Jem, boy!' – for that was his name, and a rare hand he was at fighting – and he knew me in spite of the stranger horse; and I leaned over, and stroked his head, and swore he should never be mutton. And when I was passed, he set off at full gallop, to all the rest of the J.R.'s together, and tell them young master was come home at last. (Chap. XXVII)

'Jem, boy!', the ram greeting Jan on his return home from London, by John Burgess.

I had pined so much, in the dust and heat of that great town [London], for trees, and fields, and running waters, and the sounds of country life, and the air of country winds, that never could I grow weary of those soft enjoyments ...

To awake as the summer sun came slanting over the hill-tops, with hope on every beam advance to the laughter of the morning; to see the leaves across the window ruffling on the fresh new air ... Then the lustrous meadows far beyond the thatch of the garden-wall, yet seen beneath the hanging scollops of the walnut tree, all awaking, dressed in pearl, all amazed at their own glistening ... down them troop the lowing kine, walking each with a step of character ... all alike with toss of horns,

Red Devon cattle. *A typical Exmoor farmyard.*

and spread of udders ready. From them ... we turn to the farm-yard proper ... Round it stand the snug outbuildings, barn, corn-chamber, cider-press, stables, with a blinker'd horse in every doorway munching, ... the cock ... claps his wings and shouts 'cock-a-doodle'; and no other cock dare look at him. (Chapter XXVIII)

It was very pleasant there in the copse, sloping to the west as it was, and the sun descending brightly, with rocks and banks to dwell on. The stems of mottled and dimpled wood, with twigs coming out like elbows, hung and clung together closely ... overhead the shrunken leaves quivered and rustled ripely, having many points like stars, and rising and falling delicately, as fingers play sad music. ...

All by the hedge ran a little stream, a thing that could barely name itself, flowing scarce more than a pint in a minute, because of the sunny weather ... Along and down the tiny banks, and nodding into one another ... hung the brown arcade of ferns; some with gold tongues languishing; some with countless ear-drops jerking; some with great quilled ribs uprising ... (Chapter XXXVIII)

Jan Ridd's joy at returning home from the capital knows no bounds as these extracts show. For him London is 'a very hideous and dirty place, not at all like Exmoor'. (Chapter XXIV)
    While Blackmore admitted to exaggerating the awe-inspiring qualities of the scenery around the Doone Valley 'solely for the uses of my story', the natural world enchanted him and he had a gift for conveying this feeling through his writing. In a letter to him, Thomas Hardy praised his 'exquisite ways of describing things'. For many readers Blackmore's sensitive and accurate depiction of nature in all its variety is one of the delights of the novel. Despite his 'romancing', the Exmoor he portrays is true to life.

The Sea at Lynmouth

But during those two months of fog ... the saddest and the heaviest thing was to stand by the sea. To be upon the beach yourself, and see the long waves coming in; to know that they are long waves, but only see a piece of them; and to hear them lifting roundly, swelling over smooth green rocks, plashing down in the hollow corners, but bearing on all the same as ever, soft and sleek and sorrowful, till their little noise is over.

One old man who lived at Lynmouth, seeking to be buried there, having been more than half over the world ... this old Will Watcombe ... said that our strange winter arose from a thing he called the 'Gulf-stream' rushing up channel suddenly. He said it was hot water, almost fit for a man to shave with, and it threw all our cold water out, and ruined the fish and spawning-time, and a cold spring would come after it. I was fond of going to Lynmouth on Sunday to hear this old man talk ... He told me that this powerful flood set in upon our coast so hard, sometimes once in ten years, and sometimes not for fifty ... but that when it came, therewith came warmth, and clouds, and fog, and moisture, and nuts, and fruit, and even shells ... As for nuts he winked awhile, and chewed a piece of tobacco ... afterwards I heard that nuts with liquid kernels came, travelling on the Gulf-stream; for never before was known so much foreign cordial landed upon our coast, floating ashore by mistake in the fog ... too much astray to learn its duty ... Folk ... said that Will Watcombe himself knew better than anybody else about this drift of the Gulf-stream, and the places where it would come ashore ... But De Whichehalse, our great magistrate, certified that there was no proof of unlawful importation ... And we knew that it was a foul thing for some quarrymen to say, that night after night they had been digging a new cellar at Ley Manor [De Whichehalse's house] to hold the little marks of respect found in the caverns at high-water ... We common people joked of the 'Gulp-stream', as we called it.

The sea breaking over the wall near the Rhenish Tower at Lynmouth.

(Ian Pile. © Exmoor National Park Authority).

But the thing which astonished and frightened us ... was a strange mysterious sound ... It mattered not whether you stood on the moor, or crouched behind rocks away from it ... there was rushing of something by, and melancholy laughter, and the hair of a man would stand on end ... Those who had heard it most often declared that it must

be the wail of a woman's voice, and the rustle of robes fleeing horribly, and fiends
in the fog going after her. (Chapter XII)

*Of all the western moors, only Exmoor has a coast. The sea, shipping and smuggling have
always played a large part in its story. Though the little ports – Lynmouth, Porlock Weir,
Minehead and Watchet – are not 'central' to the novel, Blackmore makes us conscious of
their presence and their influence. This passage is a good example of his skilful blending of
sea and moor when creating atmosphere, and of his use of irony in the allusion to the magistrate receiving smuggled goods. The fourteenth-century Rising Sun Inn in Lynmouth was,
according to tradition, used by smugglers.*

The Great Winter

Before Sir Ensor Doone was buried, the greatest frost of the century had set in, with its iron hand, and step of stone, on every thing ...

The strong men broke three good pickaxes, ere they got through the hard brown sod, chequed with flakes of frosty white, where old Sir Ensor was to lie upon his back, awaiting the darkness of the Judgement-day. It was in the little chapel-yard; I will not tell the name of it; because we are now such Protestants, that I might do it an evil turn ... In the very night which followed old Sir Ensor's funeral, such a storm of snow began as never have I heard nor read of ... In the bitter morning, I arose ... and saw at once that not a moment must be lost to save our stock. (Chapter XLI)

We came all safe to the lower meadow, where most of our flock was hurdled. But behold there was no flock at all! ... only at one corner of the field, by the eastern end, where the snow drove in, a great white billow, as high as a barn and as broad as a house.... Watch [the sheepdog] began to scratch at once, and to howl along the sides of it; he knew that his charge was buried there ... we four men set to in earnest, shovelling away at the great white pile, and fetching it into the meadow.

Snowdrift on Exmoor, April 2018. (© Paul Savage)

Each man made for himself a cave, scooping at the soft cold flux, which slid upon him at every stroke ... At last we drove our tunnels in ... and listened ... I laid my head well into the chamber; and there I heard a faint 'ma-a-ah' coming through some ells of snow, like a plaintive buried hope ... I shouted aloud to cheer him up ... then we all fell to again; and very soon we hauled him out ... Further in, and close under the bank, where they had huddled themselves for warmth, we found all the rest of the poor sheep packed as closely as if they were in a great pie ... Two or three of the weaklier hoggets [yearling sheep] were dead, from want of air, and from pressure; but more than three-score were as lively as ever ... (Chapter XLII)

Molly Groves standing on a snowdrift the height of Oare Post on Hookway Hill during the dreadful winter of 1962/3.
(Courtesy of Molly Groves, © Exmoor National Park Authority)

Exmoor in the snow, April 2018. (© Paul Savage)

*John Ridd rescuing two of
his sheep, by John Burgess.*

The winter of 1683–4 was one of the most severe that Britain has experienced. Rightly named the 'Great Frost', it lasted from the middle of December until the middle of February. In London, the Thames was frozen to a depth of 11 inches, and a fair was held on the ice. The writer John Evelyn noted in his diary (9 January 1684) that he went across the river 'on the ice, now become so thick as to bear not only streets of booths, in which they roasted meat, and had divers shops of wares ... but coaches, carts, and horses passed over.'

On Exmoor the ground froze to a depth of nearly four feet. Blackmore accurately depicts the conditions the gravediggers have to contend with. Before he died, Sir Ensor had given John and Lorna a grudging blessing, but their troubles are by no means over. Without the protection of Sir Ensor, Lorna is now at the mercy of the Counsellor who is determined that she marry his son, Carver. Battling his way through snow and ice, John manages, with great resourcefulness and courage, to rescue her and Gwenny and bring them both to the relative safety of Plover's Barrows.

Blackmore's personal knowledge of the realities of farming on Exmoor is used to good effect in this stirring account of the rescue of the sheep.

86

Lynmouth and Countisbury

Now ... all the towns of Somersetshire and half the towns of Devonshire were full
of pushing eager people, ready to swallow anything ... Taunton, Bridgwater,
Minehead, and Dulverton took the lead of the other towns in utterance of their
discontent, and threats of what they meant to do, if ever a Papist dared to climb
the Protestant throne of England ... So the Tory policy was to watch ... and then
to strike severely. And as a Tory watchman ... Jeremy Stickles was now among us:
and his duty was threefold. First ... to see to the levying of poundage in the little
haven of Lynmouth, and further up the coast ... Second, his duty was ... to watch
[the Doones] narrowly ... Jeremy Stickles' third business was entirely political; to
learn the temper of our people and the gentle families ... to discover any collecting
of arms and drilling of men ... to prevent ... any importation of gunpowder ... in
a word to observe and forestall the enemy. (Chapter XXXIX)

[Jeremy] agreed with me that we could not hope to escape an attack from the
outlaws, and the more especially now that they knew himself to be returned to us
... and he thought it wiser that I should go ... to Lynmouth, if a horse could pass
the valley, and fetch every one of his mounted troopers ... Knowing how fiercely
the floods were out, I resolved to travel the higher road, by Cosgate and through

Church of St John the Baptist, Countisbury.

The ancient Blue Ball Inn, Countisbury.

The precipitous cliffs below Countisbury.

Countisbury; therefore I swam my horse through the Lyn ... and thence galloped up and along the hills. I could see all the inland valleys ribboned with broad waters ... But when I descended the hill towards Lynmouth, I feared that my journey was all in vain. For the East Lyn ... was ramping and roaring frightfully, lashing whole trunks of trees on the rocks, and rending them, and grinding them ... It was certain death to attempt the passage; and the little wooden footbridge had been carried away long ago. (Chapter XLVIII)

In the extract from Chapter XXXIX Blackmore's skill in setting the Ridd–Doone story against a credible and historically-based background is evident. Only a careful reading of the book can do him justice, though. In Chapter XLVIII John makes a perilous journey to fetch help. Follow this extract on the Ordnance Survey map, his usual route would have been through Slocombeslade, Tippacott and the valley road to Lynmouth. His description of the raging Lyn reminds us of the disastrous flash flood of 15–16 August 1952 in which thirty-four people died and many houses were swept away. 'Cosgate' is County Gate. At Countisbury a fine church and inn introduce the precipitous descent into Lynmouth.

Yenworthy

For [the Doones] had a pleasant custom, when they visited farm-houses, of lighting themselves towards picking up anything they wanted, or stabbing the inhabitants, by first creating a blaze in the rickyard ... these Doones had got the worst of this pleasant trick one time. For happening to fire the ricks of a lonely farm called Yenworthy, not far above Glenthorne, they approached the house to get people's goods, and to enjoy their terror. The master of the farm was lately dead, and had left, inside the clock-case, loaded, the great long gun ... Now Widow Fisher took out this gun, and not caring much what became of her (for she had loved her husband dearly) she laid it upon the window-sill, which looked upon the rickyard; and she backed up the butt with a chest of oak drawers, and she opened the window a little back, and let the muzzle out on the slope. Presently five or six young Doones came dancing a reel ... betwixt her and the flaming rick. Upon which she

Yenworthy Farm.

Nigel Binding, the current farmer at Yenworthy, posing with the gun that Widow Fisher used to repel the Doones. He is standing in front of the window from which she first caught sight of them coming up the valley.

pulled the trigger with all the force of her thumb, and a quarter of a pound of duck-shot went out with the blaze on the dancers. You may suppose what their dancing was, and their reeling how changed to staggering, and their music none of the sweetest. One of them fell into the rick, and was burned, and buried in a ditch next day; but the others were set upon their horses, and carried home on a path of blood. And strange to say, they never avenged this very dreadful injury; but having heard that a woman had fired this desperate shot among them they said that she ought to be a Doone, and inquired how old she was. (Chapter XLVIII)

This well-known Doone tale blurs the line between legend and fact because the long gun supposedly used by Widow Fisher still exists, as the photograph shows.

    Land has been farmed at Yenworthy from medieval times and possibly earlier. There are Bronze Age barrows on Yenworthy Common. From the Common it is possible to join the South West Coast Path above Glenthorne Beach.

Exford

Not knowing that Tom Faggus has been pardoned for his highway robberies, the magistrates of Exmoor meet at Exford with their men in order to catch and shoot him. John Fry, who happens to be there at the time, brings news to Plover's Barrows of the dramatic turn of events.

For a gentleman, on a cue-ball [skewbald] horse, was coming slowly down the hill … looking at us in a friendly way … the gentleman rode up to Squire Maunder, and raised his cocked hat in a manner that took the Squire out of countenance, for he could not do the like of it.

'Sir,' he said, 'Good and worshipful sir, I am here to claim your good advice and valour; for purposes of justice. I hold His Majesty's commission, to make to cease a notorious rogue, whose name is Thomas Faggus.' With that he offered his commission; but Squire Maunder told the truth, that he could not rade [read] even words in print, much less written karacters.

… 'Your warships have posted the men right well,' saith he … 'surely that big rogue will have no chance left among so many valiant musketeers. Ha! what see I there, my friend? Rust in the pan of your gun! That gun would never go off, sure as I am the King's Commissioner. And I see another just as bad; and lo, there the third! … I fear that bold rogue would ride through all of you, and laugh at your

The centre of Exford village outside the Crown Hotel, an ideal place for the magistrates to gather.

THE LORNA DOONE TRAIL

Above: *Tom Faggus's long gun and its resting iron, held in the Barnstaple Museum.*

Left: *A close-up of the firing mechanism of Tom Faggus's gun.*

worships' beards, by George.'

'But what shall us do?' Squire Maunder axed ...

'Discharge your pieces, gentlemen, and let the men do the same ... and load again with fresh powder.'

... Thereupon they all blazed out, and the noise of it went all round the hills ...[and] the gentleman on the cue-ball horse ... out pulls two girt pistols longside of zaddle, and clap'th one to Squire Maunder's head and t'other to Sir Richard Blewitt's.

'Hand forth your money and all your warrants,' he saith like a clap of thunder; 'gentlemen, have you now the wit to apprehend Tom Faggus? ... Fust man I see go to load a gun, I'll gi'e 'un the bullet to do it with.' said Tom; for ... it was him and no other. (Chapter XXXIX)

Tom sticks the warrants in his hat, scatters the money among the bystanders and rides off. The story causes great consternation at Plover's Barrows because they fear Tom's pardon will be withdrawn. Blackmore says in a note that 'the truth of this story is well-established by first-rate tradition'. Exford is on the main east-west route between Dunster and Barnstaple, used since medieval times (now the B3224), and also on the way to South Molton via Landacre.

Watchet

A *picturesque street in Watchet.*

'How far you call it now to the bank of the sea at Wash – Wash – ?'

'At Watchet, likely you mean, madam. Oh, a very long way, and the roads as soft as the road to Oare.' (Chapter III)

Therefore ... the horses were put to again, and the heavy coach went up the hill, with the lady and her two children, and Benita sitting inside of it ... Much had been said at Dulverton, and even back at Bampton, about some great freebooters, to whom all Exmoor owed suit and service ... Through the fog, and through the muck, the coach went on ... to the pitch and the slope of the seabank, leading on towards Watchet town ... and there ... they met their fate, and could not fly it ... The silver light ... showed them ... a troop of horsemen ... ready to dash upon them ... Meanwhile the drivers drove into the sea ... But before the waves came into the coach, a score of fierce men were around it ... What followed, Benita knew not ... being stunned by a blow on the head, beside being palsied with terror ... But when she recovered her senses, she found herself upon the sand, the robbers were out of sight ... then she arose and ran to her mistress, who was sitting upright on a little rock, with her dead boy's face to her bosom, sometimes gazing upon him, and sometimes questioning round for the other one. (Chapter LIII)

And so, the John Ridd–Lorna Doone story, so fortuitously begun at an inn at Dulverton, begins to untangle its ravelled skein. Jeremy Stickles tells John of his encounter with Benita, concluding triumphantly: 'That little maid {the child abducted from the coach by the Doones} is Lorna Doone.' John's own later visit to Watchet results in a meeting between Lorna and Benita. Their recognition of each other and the network of circumstantial evidence, carefully woven by Blackmore, establishes Lorna's identity as Lady Lorna Dugal, daughter of 'a nobleman of high and goodly lineage' and of a mother 'of yet more ancient and renowned descent' (Chapter LVIII). In abducting Lorna the Doones hoped to secure her property by forcing her to marry Carver and, at the same time, to exact an exquisite revenge on the Earl of Lorne, whose daughter had been unwise enough to marry Sir Ensor Doone.

The beginnings of a storm at Watchet.
(© Paul Savage)

Present day Watchet harbour and marina.

(© Paul Savage)

St Decuman's Church, Watchet

Before the light of morning came along the tide to Watchet my Lady met her husband. They took her into the town that night, but not to her own castle; and so the power of womanhood (which is itself maternity) came over-swiftly upon her. The lady ... lies in Watchet little churchyard, with son and heir at her right hand, and a little babe ... sleeping on her bosom. (Chapter LIII)

When I heard that Lorna's father was the Earl of Dugal ... I never thought but everybody in Watchet town must know all about the tombstone of the Countess of Dugal. This however proved otherwise. For Lord Dugal had never lived at Watchet Grange; as their place was called; neither had his name become familiar as its owner ... And upon news of his death, John Jones, a rich gentleman from Llandaff, had taken possession, as next of right, and hushed up all the story ... So the poor Countess of Dugal, almost in sight of her own grand house, was buried in an unknown grave, together with her pair of infants, without a plate, without a tombstone (worse than all), without a tear, except from the hired Italian woman. Surely my poor Lorna came of an ill-starred family ... All Watchet town cared ten times as much to see John Ridd, as to show him what he wanted. I was led to every public-house, instead of to the churchyard; and twenty tables were ready for me, in lieu of a single gravestone. 'Zummerset thou bee'st, Jan Ridd, and Zummerzett thou shalt be ... Whoy, thee lives in Zummerzett; and in Zummerzett thee wast barn, lad.' and so it went on, till I was weary; though very much obliged to them. (Chapter LVI)

Having obtained from Benita ... a very close and full description of the place where her poor mistress lay, and the marks whereby to know it, I hastened to Watchet the following morning, before the sun was up, or any people were about ... In the furthest and darkest nook, overgrown with grass, and overhung by a weeping tree, a little bank of earth betokened the rounding off of a hapless life. There was nothing to tell of rank, or wealth, or love, or even pity ... I gathered a little grass for Lorna, and a sprig of the weeping tree. (Chapter LVII)

Lorna's mother was journeying to Watchet, not to take ship there but to wait at the Grange for her husband's return from abroad. In fact he had been killed falling down a precipice in the Pyrenees, but Lady Dugal could not accept this.

The hill-top church attracts many visitors – its site may have inspired Coleridge – but a search for the grave of Lorna's mother will hardly be fruitful!

St Decuman's church, Watchet, which overlooks the town.

Brendon – News of the Rebellion

When I was down, on Saturday 13th June [1685], at the blacksmith's forge by Brendon town, where the Lyn-stream runs so close that he dips his horse-shoes in it, and where the news is apt to come first of all our neighbourhood … round the corner came a man upon a pie-bald horse, looking flagged and weary. But seeing half a dozen of us, young, and brisk, and hearty, he made a flourish with his horse, and waved a blue flag vehemently, shouting with great glory –

'Monmouth, and the Protestant faith! Monmouth, and no Popery! Monmouth, the good King's eldest son! Down with the poisoning murderer! Down with the black usurper, and to the devil with all papists!'

'Why so, thou little varlet?' I asked very quietly; for the man was too small to quarrel with …

'Papist yourself, be you?' said the fellow, not daring to answer too much: 'then take this, and read it.'

The Old Forge, Brendon.

Opposite: *The East Lyn river at Brendon where it runs close to the old forge.*

And he handed me a long rigmarole, which he called a 'Declaration': I saw that it was but a heap of lies, and thrust it into the blacksmith's fire, and blew the bellows thrice at it.

... For the next fortnight, we were daily troubled with conflicting rumours ... We were told that the Duke had been proclaimed King of England, in every town of Dorset and Somerset; that he had won a great battle at Axminster ... that Taunton, and Bridgwater, and Bristowe [Bristol], were all mad with delight, the two former being in his hands, and the latter craving to be so. (Chapter LXII)

Loyal to whichever king is on the throne, John tries to avoid getting involved in the rebellion. But his sister Annie, now married to Tom Faggus, pays him a visit. Pale and tearful, she blurts out her dreadful news: Tom has gone off with the rebels, John must find him and bring him back. Following in the wake of Monmouth's army, John arrives at Sedgemoor on the morning of 6 July 1685 and witnesses the nightmarish aftermath of the battle. It is Winnie who finds John and leads him to her master, who is injured. Having bound Tom's wound, John heaves him onto Winnie and sends them home.

John himself has the misfortune to encounter Colonel Kirke's 'Lambs' (so called because their cap badge was a Paschal lamb) who hold him as a rebel. He only escapes being shot when Jeremy Stickles intervenes.

Top: *Remnants from the old forge in Brendon.*

Above: *A blacksmith's vice from the old forge in Brendon.*

As a consequence, John has to go to London once more to plead his case. There he is reunited with Lorna, who, following the discovery of her true ancestry was made a ward of Chancery and has been living with her guardian and relative, Earl Brandir. By thwarting a robbery and saving Lord Brandir's life, John comes to the notice of King James II who makes him a knight. He is also pardoned for his alleged involvement in the rebellion. Judge Jeffreys (in return for a substantial sum) releases Lorna from her wardship, and the king and queen give consent to her marriage to Sir John Ridd.

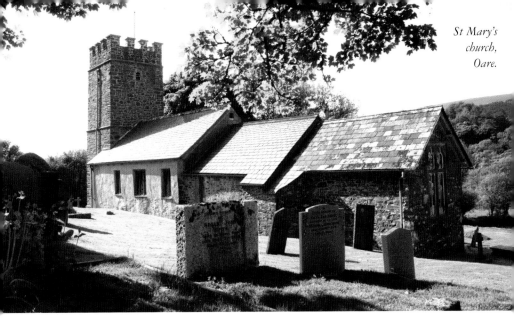

St Mary's Church, Oare

Lorna's dress was of pure white, clouded with faint lavender ... and as simple as need be, except for perfect loveliness. I was afraid to look at her ... except when each of us said, 'I will', and then each dwelled upon the other.

It is impossible for any, who have not loved as I have, to conceive my joy and pride, when after ring and all was done, and the parson had blessed us, Lorna turned to look at me, with her playful glance subdued, and deepened by this solemn act.

Her eyes, which none on earth may ever equal, or compare with, told me such a tale of hope, and faith, and heart's devotion, that I was almost amazed, thoroughly as I knew them. Darling eyes, the clearest eyes, the loveliest, the most loving eyes – the sound of a shot rang through the church, and those eyes were dim with death.

Lorna fell across my knees, when I was going to kiss her, as the bridegroom is allowed to do, and encouraged, if he needs it; a flood of blood came out upon the yellow wood of the altar steps; and at my feet lay Lorna, trying to tell me some last message out of her faithful eyes. I lifted her up, and petted her, and coaxed her, but it was no good; the only sign of life remaining was a drip of bright red blood.

Some men know what things befall them in the supreme time of their life – far above the time of death – but to me comes back as a hazy dream, without any knowledge in it, what I did, or felt, or thought, with my wife's arms flagging, flagging, round my neck, as I raised her up, and softly put them there. She sighed a long sigh on my breast, for her last farewell to life, and then she grew so cold, and cold, that I asked the time of year.

The interior of Oare church.

The Carver window, through which in the novel Carver Doone shoots Lorna Doone.

It was now Whit-Tuesday, and the lilacs all in blossom; and why I thought of the time of year, with the young death in my arms, God, or His angels, may decide ... Enough that I did, and looked; and our white lilacs were beautiful. Then I laid my wife in my mother's arms, and begging that no one would make a noise, went forth for my revenge. (Chapter LXXIV)

From the sacking of the Doone Valley and the trap set for the outlaws at the Warren, of the able-bodied men only Carver escaped. 'It was', as John says (Chapter LXII) 'no light thing to have a man of such power, and resource, and desperation, left at large and furious, like a famished wolf round the sheep-fold.' And now the wolf has preyed. When John goes forth to his revenge, unarmed, he is convinced that Lorna is dead.

A notice in Oare church draws attention to 'the Carver window', and a copy of the famous medallion portrait in Exeter Cathedral does honour to Blackmore.

It is possible that Blackmore drew on the story of the fatal shooting in 1641, in the Devon village of Chagford, of Mary Whiddon in or outside the church on her wedding day. The killer was believed to be a man she had rejected, but he was never caught.

View from the porch at Oare church in early summer.

Cloven Rocks

I came upon Black Barrow Down … and there, about a furlong before me, rode a man on a great black horse; and I knew that the man was Carver Doone … [He] turned up the gully leading from the moor to Cloven Rocks, through which John Fry had tracked Uncle Ben … But as Carver entered it, he turned round, and beheld me not a hundred yards behind; and I saw that he was bearing his child, little Ensie, before him. Ensie also descried me, and stretched his hands, and cried to me; for the face of his father frightened him …

[Carver] drew rein at the crossways sharply, and plunged into the black ravine leading to the Wizard's Slough … Now there is a way between cliff and slough, for those who know the ground thoroughly; but for him there was no road … Upon this he made up his mind; and wheeling, fired and then rode at me. His bullet struck me somewhere, but I took no heed of that. Fearing only his escape, I laid my horse across the way … Ere the slash of the sword came nigh me, man and horse rolled over … with a sullen and black scowl, the Carver gathered his mighty limbs … I think he felt that his time was come. I think he knew from my knitted muscles, and the firm arch of my breast … but most of all from my stern blue eyes, that he had found his master …

Carver Doone caught me round the waist, with such a grip as never yet had been laid upon me. I heard my rib go … then I took him by the throat … In vain he tugged, and strained, and writhed, dashed his bleeding fist into my face … I had him helpless in two minutes, and his blazing eyes lolled out… the black bog had him by the feet; the sucking of the ground drew on him, like the thirsty lips of death. In our fury, we had heeded neither wet nor dry, nor thought of the earth beneath us … He fell back … like a hummock of bog-oak, standing out of the quagmire; and then he tossed his arms to heaven, and they were black to the elbow, and the glare of his eyes was ghastly. I could only gaze and pant: for my strength was no more than an infant's from the fury and the horror. Scarcely could I turn away, while, joint by joint, he sank from sight. (Chapter LXXIV)

This famous passage has set many a reader searching for the Wizard's Slough. Blackmore gives some clues, but omits the vital ones. The chase over Black Barrow Down can be followed, but the 'crossways' and 'the black ravine' cannot be identified. Again, the killing power of this bog is not matched by any Exmoor quagmire. Cloven Rocks, if it ever tallied with this description, must have changed quite a lot, but the romantics among us may well like to think of it as the site of the dreaded Wizard's Slough.

This page and opposite: *Cloven Rocks is an area near Simonsbath, part of which is very boggy, as these two photos show, but in no way is it as treacherous as described by Blackmore in* Lorna Doone.

Happy Ending

As for Lorna ... she never tires of being with me here and there, among the beautiful places, and talking with her arm around me ... of the many fears, and troubles, dangers and discouragements, and worst of all the bitter partings, which we used to undergo.

There is no need for my farming harder than becomes a man of weight. Lorna has great stores of money, though we never draw it out, except for some poor neighbour; unless I find her a sumptuous dress, out of her own perquisites. And this she always looks upon as a wondrous gift from me; and kisses me much when she puts it on, and walks like the noble woman she is. And yet I may never behold it again; for she gets back to her simple clothes and I love her the better in them. I believe that she gives half the grandeur away, and keeps the other half for the children ...

As for poor Tom Faggus, everyone knows his bitter adventures, when his pardon was recalled, because of his sally to Sedgemoor ... [When] a new king arose ... Tom sued his pardon afresh; and Jeremy Stickles ... was glad to help him in getting it ... Thereafter, the good and respectable Tom lived a godly and righteous (though not always sober) life; and brought up his children to honesty, as the first of all qualifications.

My dear mother was as happy as possibly need be with us; having no cause for jealousy, as others arose around her ... I sent little Ensie to Blundell's School, at my own cost and charges, having changed his name, for fear of what anyone might do to him. I called him 'Ensie Jones' and I hope that he will be a credit to us ...

Of Lorna, of my lifelong darling, of my more and more loved wife, I will not talk; for it is not seemly, that a man should exalt his pride. Year by year, her beauty grows, with the growth of goodness, kindness, and true happiness – above all with loving. For change, she makes a joke of this, and plays with it, and laughs at it; and then, when my slow nature marvels, back she comes to the earnest thing. And if I wish to pay her out for something very dreadful – as may happen once or twice, when we become too gladsome – I bring her to forgotten sadness, and to me for cure of it, by the two words, 'Lorna Doone'. (Chapter LXXV)

Yes, it is a fairy-tale ending – but that, surely, is how a romance should end. Cured by Ruth's skill in medicine, Lorna is restored to John; and they live happily ever after.

Let us imagine them, as Blackmore wished us to, living their peaceful lives in the parish of Oare, in the County of Somerset: Sir John Ridd, yeoman and churchwarden, and his noble wife.

* * *

Lank Combe Water Slide.

View of Oare village in the evening sunlight.

Reading List

Blackmore, R.D., *Lorna Doone*, first published in 1869, available in a variety of editions, including abridged and audio versions.

Browne, Ida M., 'The true Story of the Doones?' reproduced and introduced by John Lerwill, accessed 7/3/18: http://www.lerwill-life.org.uk/history/doones.htm

Budd, K., *The Last Victorian: R.D. Blackmore and his novels*, London, Centaur Press, 1960.

Burton, S.H., *Exmoor*, London, Robert Hale, 1984.

Cooper, Cicely E., 'R.D. Blackmore's Other Books', *Exmoor Review*, 1973.

Cooper, T.H., *A guide containing a short historical sketch of Lynton, Lynmouth*, Barnstaple, T. Hearson, 1853. This contains stories about the Doones and about Tom Faggus. Accessed 7/3/18: https://books.google.co.uk/books/about/A_guide_containing_a_short_historical_sk.html?id=g-4GAAAAQAAJ

Dunn, W.H., *R.D. Blackmore: a biography*, London, Robert Hale, 1956.

Eardley-Wilmot, Hazel, *Yesterday's Exmoor*, Exeter, Exmoor Books, 1990. In Chapter 5 the Doones and the Monmouth Rebellion are discussed.

Hurley, Jack, *Legends of Exmoor*, Dulverton, Exmoor Press, 1973. This has a chapter on Tom Faggus.

Oakeley, A., *The facts on which R.D. Blackmore based Lorna Doone*, 3rd ed., Williton, 1973.

Rawle, E.J., *The Doones of Exmoor*, Barnicott, Taunton, 1903.

Sampson, Mike, 'Samuel Holroyd (Tim) Burton', in *Exmoor Chroniclers*, Dulverton, Exmoor Society, 2017.

Thornycroft, L.B., *The Story of the Doones in fact, fiction and photo*, Taunton, The Wessex Press, 1957.

Vowles, A., *The Doone Valley and Water-Slide*, Williton, Cox, 1929.

Wigfield, W. MacDonald, *The Monmouth Rebellion: A Social History*, Bradford-on-Avon, Moonraker Press, 1980.